Edward Spencer Beesly

Queen Elizabeth

Edward Spencer Beesly

Queen Elizabeth

ISBN/EAN: 9783337321628

Printed in Europe, USA, Canada, Australia, Japan

Cover: Foto ©ninafisch / pixelio.de

More available books at **www.hansebooks.com**

QUEEN ELIZABETH

BY

EDWARD SPENCER BEESLY

Sine ira et studio, quorum causas procul habeo.
TACITUS, ANN. I. 1.

London
MACMILLAN AND CO.
AND NEW YORK
1892

All rights reserved

FIRST EDITION PRINTED FEBRUARY 1892.
REPRINTED MARCH 1892.

Printed by T. and A. CONSTABLE, Printers to Her Majesty,
at the Edinburgh University Press.

CONTENTS

CHAPTER I
EARLY LIFE, 1533-1558 1

CHAPTER II
THE CHANGE OF RELIGION, 1559 6

CHAPTER III
FOREIGN RELATIONS, 1559-1563 18

CHAPTER IV
ELIZABETH AND MARY STUART, 1559-1568 . . . 38

CHAPTER V
ARISTOCRATIC PLOTS, 1568-1572 78

CHAPTER VI
FOREIGN AFFAIRS, 1572-1583 101

CHAPTER VII

THE PAPAL ATTACK, 1570-1583 128

CHAPTER VIII

PROTECTORATE OF THE NETHERLANDS, 1584-1586 . . 156

CHAPTER IX

EXECUTION OF THE QUEEN OF SCOTS: 1584-1587 . . 174

CHAPTER X

WAR WITH SPAIN, 1587-1603 188

CHAPTER XI

DOMESTIC AFFAIRS, 1588-1601 211

CHAPTER XII

LAST YEARS AND DEATH, 1601-1603 230

APPENDIX

	PAGE
A.—SESSIONS OF PARLIAMENT IN THE REIGN OF ELIZABETH	243
B.—PRINCIPAL HOWARDS CONTEMPORARIES OF ELIZABETH	244
C.—PRINCIPAL BOLEYN RELATIONS OF ELIZABETH	245

CHAPTER I

EARLY LIFE : 1533-1558

I HAVE to deal, under strict limitations of space, with a long life, almost the whole of its adult period passed in the exercise of sovereignty—a life which is in effect the history of England during forty-five years, abounding at the same time in personal interest, and the subject, both in its public and private aspects, of fierce and probably interminable controversies. Evidently a bird's-eye view is all that can be attempted; and the most important episodes alone can be selected for consideration.

The daughter of Henry VIII. and Anne Boleyn was born on September 6, 1533. Anne was niece of Thomas, third Duke of Norfolk, and all the great Howard kinsmen attended at the baptism four days afterwards. Elizabeth was two years and eight months old when her mother was beheaded, and she herself was declared illegitimate by Act of Parliament. It is not recorded that in after years she expressed any opinion about her mother or ever mentioned her name. She never took any steps to get the Act of attainder repealed; but perhaps she indirectly showed her belief in Anne's innocence by raising the son of Norris, her alleged paramour, to the peerage, and by the great favour she always showed to his family.

During her father's life Elizabeth lived chiefly at Hatfield with her brother Edward, under a governess. Henry had been empowered by Parliament in 1536 to settle the succession by his will. In 1544 he caused an Act to be passed placing Mary and Elizabeth next in order of succession after Edward. By his will, made a few days before his death, he repeated the provisions of the Act of 1544, and placed next to Elizabeth the daughters of his younger sister, the Duchess of Suffolk, tacitly passing over his elder sister, the Queen of Scotland.

After her father's death (Jan. 1547) Elizabeth, then a girl of thirteen, went to reside with the Queen Dowager Catherine, who had not been many weeks a widow before she married her old lover Thomas Seymour, the Lord Admiral, brother of the Protector Somerset, described as "fierce in courage, courtly in fashion, in personage stately, in voice magnificent, but somewhat empty of matter." The romping that soon began to go on between this dangerous man and Elizabeth was of such a nature that early in the next year Catherine found it necessary to send her away somewhat abruptly. From that time she resided chiefly at Hatfield.

In August 1548 Catherine died, and the Admiral at once formed the project of marrying Elizabeth. This and other ambitious designs brought him to the scaffold (March 1549). It does not appear that Elizabeth saw or directly corresponded with him after he was a widower. But she listened to his messages, and dropped remarks of an encouraging kind which she meant to be repeated to him. She knew perfectly well that the marriage would not be permitted. She was only flirting with a man old enough to be her father just as she afterwards flirted with men young enough to be her sons. We already get a glimpse of the utter absence both of delicacy and depth of feeling which characterised her through life. When she heard of the Admiral's execution she simply remarked, "This day died a man with much wit and very little judgment." With Elizabeth the heart never really spoke, and if the senses did, she had them under perfect control. And this was why she never loved or was loved, and never has been or will be regarded with enthusiasm by either man or woman. For some time after this scandal she was evidently somewhat under a cloud. She lived at her manor-houses of Ashridge, Enfield, and Hatfield, diligently pursuing her studies under the celebrated scholar Ascham.

When Edward died (July 6, 1553) Elizabeth was nearly twenty. Although Mary's cause was her own, she remained carefully neutral during the short queenship of Jane. On its collapse she hastened to congratulate her sister, and rode by her side when she made her entry into London. During the early part of Mary's reign her life hung by a thread. The slightest indiscretion would have been fatal to her. Wyatt's insurrection was made avowedly in her favour. But neither to that nor any other conspiracy did she extend the smallest encouragement. Her prudent and blameless conduct gave her the more right in after years to deal severely with Mary Stuart, whose behaviour under precisely similar circumstances was so very different.

Renard, the Spanish ambassador, demanded her execution as the condition of the Spanish match, and Mary assured him that she would do her best to satisfy him. In the time of Henry VIII. such an intention on the part of the sovereign would have been equivalent to a sentence of death. But Mary was far from being as powerful as her father. The Council had to be reckoned with, and in the Council independent and even peremptory language was now to be heard. It was not without strong protests on the part of some of the Lords that Elizabeth was sent to the Tower. Sussex, a noble of the old blood, who was charged to conduct her there, took upon him to delay her departure, that she might appeal to the Queen for an interview. Mary was furious: "For their lives," she said, "they durst not have acted so in her father's time; she wished he was alive and among them for a single month." But it was usless to storm. The absolute monarchy had seen its best days. Sussex, fearing foul play, warned the Lieutenant of the Tower to keep within his written instructions. Howard of Effingham, the Lord Admiral, had done more than any one else to place Mary on the throne. But he was Elizabeth's great-uncle, and he angrily insisted that her food in the Tower should be prepared by her own servants. A proposal in Parliament to give the Queen the power to nominate a successor was received with such disfavour that it had to be withdrawn. Finally the judges declared that there was no evidence to convict Elizabeth. Sullenly therefore the Queen had to give way.

Elizabeth was sent to Woodstock, where she resided for about a year under guard. This was only reasonable. An heir to the throne, in whose favour there had been plots, could not expect complete freedom. In October 1555 she was allowed to go to Hatfield under the surveillance of Sir Thomas Pope. During the rest of the reign she escaped molestation by outward conformity to the Catholic religion, and by taking no part whatever in politics. But as it became clear that her accession was at hand there can be no doubt that she was engaged in studying the problems with which she would have to deal. She was already in close intimacy with Cecil, and it is evident that she mounted the throne with a policy carefully thought out in its main lines.

When Mary was known to be dying, the Spanish ambassador, Feria, called on Elizabeth, and told her that his master had exerted his influence with the Queen and Council on her behalf, and had secured her succession. But she declined to be patronised, and told him that the people and nobility were on her side.

CHAPTER II

THE CHANGE OF RELIGION : 1559

MARY died on the 17th of November 1558. Parliament was then sitting, and, in communicating the event to both Houses, Archbishop Heath frankly took the initiative in recognising Elizabeth, " of whose most lawful right and title in the succession of the Crown, thanks be to God, we need not to doubt." He was a staunch Catholic, and two months later refused to officiate at her coronation. But he was an Englishman, and even the most convinced Catholics, though looking forward with uneasiness to the religious policy of the new Queen, were sincerely glad that there was no danger of a disputed succession. Besides, it was by no means clear that Elizabeth would not accept the ecclesiastical constitution as established in the late reign. That there would be an end of burnings, and of the harassing tyranny of the bishops, every one felt certain ; but it seemed quite upon the cards that Elizabeth would continue to recognise the headship of the Pope in a formal way and maintain the Mass. It must be remembered that the religious changes had only begun some thirty years before. All middle-aged men could remember the time when the ecclesiastical fabric stood to all appearance unbroken, as it had stood for centuries. Only twenty-four years had passed since the Act of Supremacy had transferred the headship of the Church from the Pope to the King; only eleven since the Protestant doctrine and worship had been forced on the country by the Protector Somerset, to the horror and disgust of the great majority of Englishmen. The nation had sorrowed for the death of Edward VI., because it darkened the prospects of the succession, and seemed likely sooner or later to bring on a civil war. But apart from the hot Protestant minority, chiefly to be found in London, the mass of the nation was conservative, and welcomed the re-establishment of the old religion as a return to order and common sense after a short and bitter experience of revolutionary anarchy. There was a rooted objection to restore the old meddlesome tyranny of the bishops, and the nobles and squires who had got hold of the abbey lands would not hear of giving them up. But the return to communion with the Catholic Church and the recognition of the Pope as its head gave satisfaction to three-fourths, perhaps to five-sixths, of the nation, and to a still larger proportion of its most influential class, the great landed proprietors. Mary's accession was the great and unique opportunity for the old Church. If Mary and Pole had been cool-headed politicians instead of excitable fanatics, if they had contented themselves with restoring the old worship, depriving the few Protestant clergy of their benefices, and punishing only outrageous attacks on the State religion, Elizabeth would not have had the power, it may be doubted whether she would have had the inclination, to undo her sister's work.

This great opportunity was thrown away. Mary's bishops came back brooding over the long catalogue of humiliations and indignities which their Church had suffered, and thirsting to avenge their own wrongs. For six years they had their fling, and contrived to make the country forget the period of Protestant misgovernment. England had never before known what it was to be governed by clergymen. It was a sort of rule as hateful to most Catholic laymen as to Protestants. Catholics therefore for the most part, as well as Protestants, hailed the accession of Elizabeth. At any rate there would be an end of the clerical tyranny. Nor were they without hope that she would maintain the old worship. She had conformed to it for the last five years, and Philip had given the word that she was to be supported.

We are now accustomed to the Papal *non possumus*. No nation or Church can hope that the smallest deviation from Roman doctrine or discipline will be tolerated. But in 1558 the hard and fast line had not yet been drawn. France was still pressing for such changes as communion in both kinds, worship in the vulgar tongue, and marriage of priests. The Council of Trent, it is true, had already in 1545 decided that Catholic doctrine was contained in the Bible *and tradition*, and in 1551 had defined transubstantiation and the sacraments. But in 1552 the Council was prorogued, and it did not resume till 1562. Doctrine and discipline therefore might be, and were still considered to be, in the melting-pot, and no one could be certain what would come out. If Elizabeth had contented herself with the French programme, and had joined France in pressing it, the other sovereigns, who really cared for nothing but uniformity, would probably have forced the Pope to compromise. The Lutheran doctrine of consubstantiation might have been tolerated. The Anglican formulæ have been held by many to be compatible with a belief in the Real Presence. The formal severance of England from Catholic unity might thus have been postponed—possibly avoided—in the same sense that it has been avoided in France. After the completion of the Council of Trent (1562-3) it was too late.

Two years after her accession Elizabeth told the Spanish ambassador, De Quadra, that her belief was the belief of all the Catholics in the realm; and on his asking her how then she could have altered religion in 1559, she said she had been compelled to act as she did, and that, if he knew how she had been driven to it, she was sure he would excuse her. Seven years later she made the same statement to De Silva. Elizabeth was habitually so regardless of truth that her assertions can be allowed little weight when they are improbable. No doubt, as a matter of taste and feeling, she preferred the Catholic worship. She was not pious. She was not troubled with a tender conscience or tormented by a sense of sin. She did not care to cultivate close personal relations with her God. A religion of form and ceremony suited her better. But her training had been such as to free her from all superstitious fear or prejudice, and her religious convictions were determined by her sense of what was most reasonable and convenient. There is not the least evidence that she was a reluctant agent in the adoption of Protestantism in 1559. Who was there to coerce her? The Protestants could not have set up a Protestant competitor. The great nobles, though opposed to persecution and desirous of minimising the Pope's authority, would have preferred to leave worship as it was. But upon one thing Elizabeth was determined. She would resume the full ecclesiastical supremacy which her father had annexed to the Crown. She judged, and she probably judged rightly, that the only way to assure this was to make the breach with the old religion complete. If she had placed herself in the hands of moderate Catholics like Paget, possessed with the belief that she could only maintain herself by the protection of Philip, they would have advised her to be content with the practical authority over the English Church which many an English king had known how to exercise. That was not enough for her. She desired a position free from all ambiguity and possibility of dispute, not one which would have to be defended with constant vigilance and at the cost of incessant bickering.

From the point of view of her foreign relations the moment might seem to be a dangerous one for carrying out a religious revolution, and many a statesman with a deserved reputation for prudence would have counselled delay. But this disadvantage was more than counterbalanced by the unpopularity which the cruelties and disasters of Mary's last three years had brought upon the most active Catholics. Again, Elizabeth no doubt recognised that the Catholics, though at present the strongest, were the declining party. The future was with the Protestants. It was the young men who had fixed their hopes upon her in her sister's time, and who were ready to rally round her now. By her natural disposition, and by her culture, she belonged to the Renaissance rather than to the Reformation. But obscurantist as Calvinism essentially was, the Calvinists, as a minority struggling for freedom to think and teach what they believed, represented for a time the cause of light and intellectual emancipation. Was she to put herself at the head of reaction or progress? She did not love the Calvinists. They were too much in earnest for her. Their narrow creed was as tainted with superstition as that of Rome, and, at bottom, was less humane, less favourable to progress. But whom else had she to work with? The reasonable, secular-minded, tolerant sceptics are not always the best fighting material; and at that time they were few in number and tending—in England at least—to be ground out of existence between the upper and nether millstones of the rival fanaticisms. If she broke with Catholicism she would be sure of the ardent and unwavering support of one-third of the nation ; so sure, that she would have no need to take any further pains to please them. As for the remaining two-thirds, she hoped to conciliate most of them by posing as their protector against the persecution which would have been pleasing to Protestant bigots.

In the policy of a complete breach with Rome, Cecil was disposed to go as far as the Queen, and further. Cecil was at this time thirty-eight. For forty years he continued to be the confidential and faithful servant of Elizabeth. One of those new men whom the Tudors most trusted, he was first employed by Henry VIII. Under Edward he rose to be Secretary of State, and was a pronounced Protestant. On the fall of his patron Somerset he was for a short time sent to the Tower, but was soon in office again—sooner, some thought, than was quite decent—under his patron's old enemy, Northumberland. He signed the letters-patent by which the crown was conferred on Lady Jane Grey; but took an early opportunity of going over to Mary. During her reign he conformed to the old religion, and, though not holding any office, was consulted on public business, and was one of the three commissioners who went to fetch Cardinal Pole to England. Thoroughly capable in business, one of those to whom power naturally falls because they know how to use it, a shrewd balancer of probabilities, without a particle of fanaticism in his composition and detesting it in others, though ready to make use of it to serve his ends, entirely believing that "whate'er is best administered is best," Cecil nevertheless had his religious predilections, and they were all on the side of the Protestants. Moreover he had a personal motive which, by the nature of the case, was not present to the Queen. She might die prematurely; and if that event should take place before the Protestant ascendancy was firmly established his power would be at an end, and his very life would be in danger. A time came when he and his party had so strengthened themselves, if not in absolute numerical superiority, yet by the hold they had established on all departments of Government from the highest to the lowest, that they were in a condition to resist a Catholic claimant to the throne, if need were, sword in hand. But during the early years of the reign Cecil was working with the rope round his neck. Hence he could not regard the progress of events with the imperturbable *sang-froid* which Elizabeth always displayed; and all his influence was employed to push the religious revolution through as rapidly and completely as possible.

The story that Elizabeth was influenced in her attitude to Rome by an arrogant reply from Pope Paul IV. to her official notification of her accession, though refuted by Lingard and Hallam in their later editions, has been repeated by recent historians. Her accession was notified to every friendly sovereign except the Pope. He was studiously ignored from the first. Equally unsupported by facts are all attempts to show that during the early weeks of her reign she had not made up her mind as to the course she would take about religion. All preaching, it is true, was suspended by proclamation; and it was ordered that the established worship should go on "until consultation might be had in Parliament by the Queen and the three Estates." In the meantime she had herself crowned according to the ancient ritual by the Catholic Bishop of Carlisle. But this is only what might have been expected from a strong ruler who was not disposed to let important alterations be initiated by popular commotion or the presumptuous forwardness of individual clergymen. The impending change was quite sufficiently marked from the first by the removal of the most bigoted Catholics from the

Council and by the appointment of Cecil and Bacon to the offices of Secretary and of Lord Keeper. The new Parliament, Protestant candidates for which had been recommended by the Government, met as soon as possible (Jan. 25, 1559). When it rose (May 8th) the great change had been legally and decisively accomplished.

The government, worship, and doctrine of the Established Church are the most abiding marks left by Elizabeth on the national life of England. Logically it might have been expected that the settlement of doctrine would precede that of government and worship. It is characteristic of a State Church that the inverse order should have been followed. For the Queen the most important question was Church government; for the people, worship. Both these matters were disposed of with great promptitude at the beginning of 1559. Doctrine might interest the clergy; but it could wait. The Thirty-nine Articles were not adopted by Convocation till 1563, and were not sanctioned by Parliament till 1571.

The government of the Church was settled by the Act of Supremacy (April 1559). It revived the Act of Henry VIII., except that the Queen was styled Supreme Governor of the Church instead of Supreme Head, although the nature of the supremacy was precisely the same. The penalties were relaxed. Henry's oath of supremacy might be tendered to any subject, and to decline it was high treason; Elizabeth's oath was to be obligatory only on persons holding spiritual or temporal office under the Crown, and the penalty for declining was the loss of such office. Those who chose to *attack* the supremacy were still liable to the penalties of treason on the third offence.

Worship was settled with equal expedition by the Act of Uniformity (April 1559), which imposed the second or more Protestant Prayer-book of Edward VI., but with a few very important alterations. A deprecation in the Litany of "the tyranny of the Bishop of Rome and all his detestable enormities," and a rubric which declared that by kneeling at the Communion no adoration was intended to any real and essential presence of Christ, were expunged. The words of administration in the present communion service consist of two sentences. The first sentence, implying real presence, belonged to Edward's first Prayer-book; the second, implying mere commemoration, belonged to his second Prayer-book. The Prayer-book of 1559 simply pieced the two together, with a view to satisfy both Catholics and Protestants. Lastly, the vestments prescribed in Edward's first Prayer-book were retained till further notice. These alterations of Edward's second Prayer-book, all of them designed to propitiate the Catholics, were dictated by Elizabeth herself. In all this legislation Convocation was entirely ignored. Both its houses showed themselves strongly Catholic. But their opinion was not asked, and no notice was taken of their remonstrances.

While determining that England should have a purely national Church, and for that reason casting in her lot with the Protestants, Elizabeth, as we have seen, made very considerable sacrifices of logic and consistency in order to induce Catholics to conform. Like a strong and wise statesman, she did not allow herself to be driven into one concession after another, but went at once as far as she intended to go. At the same time the coercion applied to the Catholics, while sufficient to influence the worldly-minded majority, was, during the early part of her reign, very mild for those times. She wished no one to be molested who did not go out of his way to invite it. Outward conformity was all she wanted. And of this mere attendance at church was accepted as sufficient evidence. The principal difficulty, of course, was with the clergy. From them more than a mere passive conformity had to be exacted. To sign declarations, take oaths, and officiate in church was a severer strain on the conscience. It is said that less than 200 out of 9400 sacrificed their benefices rather than conform, and that of these about 100 were dignitaries. The number must be under-stated ; for the chief difficulty of the new bishops, for a long time, was to find clergymen for the parish churches. But we cannot doubt that the large majority of the parish clergy stuck to their livings, remaining Catholics at heart, and avoiding, where they could, and as long as they could, compliance with the new regulations. It must not be supposed that the enactment of religious changes by Parliament was equivalent, as it would be at the present day, to their immediate enforcement throughout the country; especially in the north where the great proprietors and justices of the peace did not carry out the law. A certain number of the ejected priests continued to celebrate the ancient rites privately in the houses of the more earnest Catholics; for which they were not unfrequently punished by imprisonment.

Of course this was persecution. But according to the ideas of that day it was a very mild kind of persecution; and where it occurred it seems to have been due to the zeal of some of the bishops, and to private busybodies who set the law in motion, rather than to any systematic action on the part of the Government.

CHAPTER III

FOREIGN RELATIONS: 1559-1563

THE successful wars waged by Edward III. and Henry V. are apt to cause an exaggerated estimate of the strength of England under the Tudors. The population—Wales included—was probably not much more than four millions. That of France was perhaps four times as large, and the superiority in wealth was even greater.[1] Before the reign of Louis XI., France, weakened by feudal disunion, had been an easy prey to her smaller but better-organised neighbour. The work of concentration effected by the greatest of French kings towards the close of the fifteenth century, and the simultaneous rise of the great Spanish empire, caused England to fall at once into the rank of a second-rate power. Such she really was under Henry VIII., notwithstanding the rather showy figure he managed to make by adhering alternately to Charles V. and Francis I. Under the bad government of Edward and Mary the fighting strength of England declined not only relatively, but absolutely, until in the last

[1] Mr. Motley conjectures that the population of Spain and Portugal may have been 12,000,000.

year of Mary it touched the lowest point in our history. Although we were at war with France, there were no soldiers, no officers, no arms, no fortresses that could resist artillery, few ships, a heavy debt, and deep discouragement. The loss of Calais, which had been held for 200 years, was the simple and natural consequence of this prostration. Justice will not be done to the great recovery under Elizabeth unless we understand how low the country had sunk when she came to the throne.

During the early years of her reign, it was the universal opinion at home and abroad that without Spanish protection she could not preserve her throne against a French invasion in the interests of Mary Stuart. Henry II. meant that, by the marriage of the Dauphin Francis with Mary, the kingdoms of England and Scotland should be united to one another and eventually to France. Philip would thus lose the command of the sea route to the Netherlands, and the hereditary duel with the House of Austria would be decided. This scheme could not seem fantastic in a century which had seen such immense agglomerations of territory effected by political marriages. Philip, on the other hand, made sure that the danger from France must necessarily throw Elizabeth and England into his arms. Notwithstanding the warnings he received from his ambassador Feria that Elizabeth was a heretic, he felt certain that she would not venture to alter religion at the risk of offending him. The only question with him was whether he should marry her himself or bestow her on some sure friend of his house. That she would refuse both himself and his nominee was a contingency he never contemplated.

Elizabeth, from the first, made up her mind that the cards in her hand could be played to more advantage than Philip supposed. England, no doubt, needed his protection for the present. But could he please himself about granting it? Her bold calculation was that his own interests would compel him, in any case, to prevent the execution of the Stuart-Valois scheme, and that consequently she might settle religion without reference to his wishes.

The offer of marriage came in January 1559. In his letter to Feria, Philip spoke as if Elizabeth would of course jump at it. After dwelling on its many inconveniences, he said he had decided to make the sacrifice on condition that Elizabeth would uphold the Catholic religion; but she must not expect him to remain long with her; he would visit England occasionally. Feria foolishly allowed this letter to be seen, and the contents were reported to Elizabeth. She was as much amused as piqued. Their ages were not unsuitable. Philip was thirty-two, and Elizabeth was twenty-five. But she was as fastidious about men as her father was about women; and for no political consideration would she have tied herself to her ugly, disagreeable, little brother-in-law. After some fencing, she replied that she did not mean to marry, and that she was not afraid of France.

Before the death of Mary, negotiations for a peace between France, Spain, and England had already begun. Calais was almost the only difficulty remaining to be settled. Our countrymen have never been able to understand how their possession of a fortress within the natural boundaries of another country can be disagreeable to its inhabitants. Elizabeth shared the national feeling, and she wanted Philip to insist on the restitution of Calais. He would have done so if she had pleased him as to other matters. Even as it was, the presence of a French garrison in Calais was so inconvenient to the master of the Netherlands that he was ready to fight on if England would do her part. But Elizabeth would only promise to fight Scotland—a very indirect and, indeed, useless way of supporting Philip. When once this point was made clear, peace was soon concluded between the three powers at Câteau, near Cambray (March 1559); appearances being saved by a stipulation that Calais should be restored in eight years, or half a million of crowns be forfeited.

In thus giving way Elizabeth showed her good sense. To have fought on would have meant deeper debt, terrible exhaustion, and, what was worse, dependence on Philip. Moreover, Calais could only have been recovered by reducing France to helplessness, which would have been fatal to the balance of power on which Elizabeth relied to make herself independent of both her great neighbours. The peace of Câteau Cambresis was attended with a secret compact between Philip II. and Henry II., that each monarch should suppress heresy in his own dominions and not encourage it in those of his neighbour. By the accession of Elizabeth, and the Scotch Reformation which immediately followed, Protestantism reached its high-water mark in Europe. The long wars of Charles V.

with France had enabled it to spread. Francis I. had intrigued with the Protestant princes of the Empire, and Charles had been obliged to humour them. Protestantism was victorious in Britain, Scandinavia, North Germany, the Palatinate, and Swabia. It had spread widely in Poland, Hungary, the Netherlands, and France. This rapid growth was now about to be checked. In some of these countries the new religion was destined to succumb; in some entirely to disappear. Men who could remember the first preachings of Luther lived to see not only the high-water, but the ebb, of the Protestant tide. The revolutionary tendencies inherent in Protestantism began to alarm the sovereigns; and all the more because the Church in Catholic, hardly less than in Protestant, countries was becoming a department of the State. Kings had been jealous of the spiritual power when it belonged to the Popes. They became jealous for it when it was annexed to the throne.

Notwithstanding its secret stipulations, the peace of Câteau Cambresis relieved England from the most pressing and immediate perils by which she was threatened. Neither French nor Spanish troops had made their appearance on our soil. A breathing-time at least had been gained, during which something might be done towards putting the country in a state of defence, and restoring the finances.

But the danger from France was by no means at an end. In the treaty with England, the title of Elizabeth had been acknowledged. But in that with Spain, the Dauphin had styled himself "King of Scotland, England, and Ireland." He and Mary had also assumed the English arms. If a French army invaded England, it would come by way of Scotland. The English Catholics, who had for the most part frankly accepted the succession of Elizabeth, were disappointed and irritated by the change of religion. If Mary should go to Scotland with a French force, it was to be apprehended that a rebellion would immediately break out in the northern counties. Philip, no doubt, would land in the south to drive out the Dauphiness. But the remedy would be worse than the disease. For he was deeply discontented with the conduct of Elizabeth, and would probably take the opportunity of deposing her. To establish, therefore, her independence of both her powerful neighbours, Elizabeth had to begin by destroying French influence in Scotland.

The wisest heads in Scotland had long seen the advantage of uniting their country to England by marriage. The blundering and bullying policy of the Protector Somerset had driven the Scotch to renew their ancient alliance with France. But the attempts of the Regent Mary of Guise to increase French influence, and to establish a small standing army, in order at once to strengthen her authority, and to serve the designs of Henry II. against England, had again made the French connection unpopular, and caused a corresponding revival of friendly feeling towards England.

Nowhere was the Church so wealthy, relatively to the other estates, as in Scotland. It was supposed to possess half the property of the country. Nowhere were the clergy so immoral. Nowhere was superstition so gross. But the doctrines of the Reformation were spreading among the common people, and in 1557 some of the nobles, hungering for the wealth of the Church, put themselves at the head of the Protestant movement. They were known as the "Lords of the Congregation."

The Scotch Reformation began not from the Government, as in England, but from the people. Hence, while change of supremacy was the main question in England, change of doctrine and worship took the lead in Scotland. The two parties were about equal in numbers, the Protestants being strongest in the Lowlands. But, with the exception of the murder of Beaton in 1546, there had, as yet, been no appeal to force, nor any attempt to procure a public change of religion. The accession of Elizabeth emboldened the Protestants. At Perth they took possession of the churches and burnt a monastery. On the other hand, after the peace of Câteau Cambresis, Henry II. directed the Regent to put down Protestantism, both in pursuance of the agreement with Philip, and in order to prepare for the Franco-Scottish invasion of England. The result was that the Protestants rose in open rebellion (June 1559). The Lords of the Congregation occupied Perth, Stirling, and Edinburgh. All over the Lowlands abbeys were wrecked, monks harried, churches cleared of images, the Mass abolished, and King Edward's service established in its place. In England the various changes of religion in the last thirty years had always been effected legally by King and Parliament. In Scotland the Catholic Church was overthrown by a simultaneous popular outbreak.

The catastrophe came later than in England; but popular feeling was more prepared for it; and what was now cast down was never set up again.

It seemed at first as if the Regent and her handful of regular troops, commanded by d'Oysel, would be swept away. But d'Oysel had fortified Leith, and was even able to take the field. A French army was expected. The tumultuary forces of the needy Scotch nobles could not be kept together long, and it became clear that, unless supported by Elizabeth, the rebellion would be crushed as soon as the French reinforcements should arrive, if not sooner.

Thus early did Elizabeth find herself confronted by the Scottish difficulty, which was to cause her so much anxiety throughout the greater part of her reign. The problem, though varying in minor details, was always essentially the same. There was a Protestant faction looking for support to England, and a Catholic faction looking to France. Two or three of the Protestant leaders—Moray, Glencairn, Kirkaldy—did really care something about a religious reformation. The rest thought more of getting hold of Church lands and pursuing old family feuds. In the experience of Elizabeth, they were a needy, greedy, treacherous crew, always sponging on her treasury, and giving her very little service in return for her money. Besides, the whole Scotch nation was so touchy in its patriotism, so jealous of foreign interference, that foreign soldiers present on its soil were sure to be regarded with an evil eye, no matter for what purpose they had come, or by whom they had been invited.

The Lords of the Congregation invoked the protection of Elizabeth. They suggested that she should marry the Earl of Arran, and that he and she should be King and Queen of Great Britain. Arran was the eldest son of the Duke of Chatelherault, who, Mary being as yet childless, was heir-presumptive to the Scottish crown. There were many reasons why Elizabeth should decline interference. It was throwing down the glove to France. Interference in Scotland had always been disastrous. It might drive the English Catholics to despair, as cutting off the hope of Mary's succession to the English crown. To make a Protestant match would irritate Philip. He might invade England to forestall the French. Almost all her Council—even Bacon—advised her to leave Scotland alone, marry the Archduke Charles, and trust to the Spanish alliance for the defence of England.

These were serious considerations; and to them was to be joined another which with Elizabeth always had great weight—more, naturally, than it had with any of her advisers. ⌈She shrank from doing anything which might have the practical effect of weakening the common cause of monarchs. She felt instinctively that with Protestants reverence for the religious basis of kingship must tend to become weaker than with Catholics. She did not desire to encourage this tendency or to familiarise her own subjects with it.⌋ Knox's *First Blast of the Trumpet against the Monstrous Regimen of Women* had been directed against Mary. The Blasts that were to follow had been dropped; but the first could not be treated as unblown. And the arrogant preacher did not mend matters by writing to Elizabeth that she was to consider her case as an exception "contrary to nature," allowed by God "for the comfort of His kirk," but that if she based her title on her birth or on law, "her felicity would be short."

Nevertheless Elizabeth adopted the bolder course. The Lords of the Congregation were assured that England would not see them crushed by French arms. A small supply of money was sent to them. As to the marriage with Arran, no positive answer was given; but he was sent for to be looked at. When he came, he was found to be even a poorer creature than his father; at times, indeed, not quite right in his mind. It was hard upon the Hamiltons, among whom were so many able and daring men, that, with the crown almost in their grasp, their chiefs should be such incapables. To Elizabeth it was no doubt a relief to find that Arran was an impossible husband.

In the meantime 2000 French had arrived, and the Lords were urgent in their demands for help. But Elizabeth determined, and rightly, that they must do their own work if they could. She was willing to give them such pecuniary help as was necessary. But the demand for troops was unreasonable. Fighting men abounded in Scotland. Why should English troops be sent to do their fighting for them, with the certainty of earning black looks rather than thanks? If a large army was despatched from France, she would attack it with her fleet. If it landed, she would send an English army. But if the Lords of the Congregation did not beat the handful of Frenchmen at Leith it must be because they were either weak or treacherous. In either case Elizabeth might have to give up the policy she preferred, leave Scotland alone, and fall back upon an alliance with Philip.

In order therefore to preserve this second string to her bow, and to let the Scotch Anglophiles see that she possessed it, she reopened negotiations for the Austrian marriage. Charles, in his turn, was invited to come and be looked at. Much as she disliked the idea of marriage, she knew that political reasons might make it necessary. But, come what would, she would never marry a man who was not to her fancy as a man. She would take no one on the strength of his picture. She had heard that Charles was not over-wise, and that he had an extraordinarily big head, " bigger than the Earl of Bedford's."

The Scotch Lords, finding that Elizabeth was determined to have some solid return for her money, went to work with more vigour. They proclaimed the deposition of the Regent, drove her from Edinburgh, and besieged her and her French garrison in Leith. But this burst of energy was soon over. The Protestants were more ready to pull down images and harry monks than make campaigns. Leith was not to be taken. In three weeks their army dwindled away, and the little disciplined force of Frenchmen re-entered Edinburgh.

The position had become very critical for Elizabeth. A French army of 15,000 men was daily expected at Leith. If once it landed, the Congregation would be crushed; the Hamiltons would make their peace; and the disciplined army of d'Elbœuf, swelled by hordes of hungry Scotchmen, would pour over the Border, and proclaim Mary in the midst of the Catholic population which ten years later rose in rebellion under the northern Earls.

In this difficulty the Spanish Ministers in the Netherlands were consulted. If Elizabeth expelled the garrison at Leith, and so brought upon herself a war with France, could she depend on Philip's assistance? The reply was menacing. Their master, for his own interest, could not allow the Queen of France and Scotland to enforce her title to the throne of England. But he would oppose it in his own way. If a French army entered England from the north, a Spanish army would land on the south coast. Turning to her own Council for advice, Elizabeth found no encouragement. They recommended her to take Philip's advice, and even to retrace some of her steps in the matter of religion in order to propitiate him. She made a personal appeal to the Duke of Norfolk to take the command of the forces on the Border. But he declined to be the instrument of a policy which he disapproved.

We need not wonder if Elizabeth hesitated for a while. Some of these councillors were not too well affected to her. But most of them were thoroughly loyal, and there was really much to be said for the more cautious policy. She herself was an eminently cautious politician, inclined by nature to shrink from risky courses. Never, therefore, in her whole career did she give greater proof of her large-minded comprehension of the main lines of policy which it behoved her to follow than when she determined to override the opinions of so many prudent advisers, and expel the French force from the northern kingdom.

England was not quite in the helpless, disabled position that it pleased the Spaniards to believe. Twelve months of careful and energetic administration had already done wonders. There had been wise economy and wise expenditure. Money had been scraped together, and, though there was still a heavy debt, the legacy of three wasteful reigns, the confidence of the Antwerp money-lenders had revived, and they were willing to advance considerable sums. A fleet had been equipped and manned; shiploads of arms had been imported; forces had been collected on the south coasts. The Border garrisons had been quietly raised in strength till they were able to furnish an expeditionary force at a moment's notice.

The smallest energy on the part of the Congregation might have finished the war without the presence of an English force. Elizabeth had a right to be angry. The Scotch Protestants expected to have the hardest part of the work done for them, and to be paid for executing their own share of it. Lord James and a few of the leaders were in earnest, but others were selfish time-servers. As for the lower class, their Calvinism was still new. It had not yet bred that fierce spirit of independence which before long was to outweigh the force of nobles and gentry. But if the weakness of the Anglophile party was disappointing, it had at all events shown that Elizabeth must depend upon herself to ward off danger on that side; and after some reasonable hesitation she decided to put through the work she had begun.

It says much for the patriotism of Elizabeth's Council that when they found she had made up her mind they did not stand sulkily aloof, but co-operated heartily and vigorously in carrying out the policy they had opposed. Norfolk himself accepted the command of the Border army, and acted throughout the affair with fidelity and diligence. He was not a man distinguished by ability of any kind, and the actual fighting was to be done by Lord Grey, a firm and experienced, though not brilliant, commander. But that the natural leader of the Conservative nobility should be seen at the head of Elizabeth's army was a useful lesson to traitors at home and enemies abroad, who were telling each other that her throne was insecure.

An agreement between the English Queen and the Lords of the Congregation was drawn up (February 27), with scrupulous care to avoid the appearance of dictation and encroachment which had gathered all Scotland to Pinkie Cleugh eleven years before. It set forth that the English troops were entering Scotland for no other object than to assist the Duke of Chatelherault, the heir-presumptive to the throne, and the other nobles, to drive out the foreign invaders. They would build no fortress. There was no intention to prejudice Mary's lawful authority. Cecil appears to have wanted to add something about "Christ's true religion;" but Elizabeth struck it out. Circumstances might compel her to be the protector of foreign Protestants; but neither then nor at any other time did she desire to pose in that character.

A month later (March 28th) Lord Grey crossed the Border, and marched to Leith. The siege of that place proved to be tedious. The Lords of the Congregation gave very insufficient assistance; and, when an assault had been repulsed with heavy loss, the citizens of Edinburgh would not receive the wounded into their houses. At last, when food was running short in the town, an envoy from France arrived with power to treat on behalf of the Queen of Scots. Her mother, the Regent, had died during the siege. After much haggling a treaty was signed. No French troops were in future to be kept in Scotland. Offices of State were to be held only by natives. The government during Mary's absence was to be vested in a Council of twelve noblemen; seven nominated by her and five by the Estates. Elizabeth's title to the kingdoms of England and Ireland was recognised (July 1560).

Such was the Treaty of Edinburgh, or of Leith, as it is sometimes called, one of the most successful achievements of a successful reign. It was gained by wise counsel and bold resolve; and its fruits, though not completely fulfilling its promise, were solid and valuable. It was not ratified by Mary. But her non-ratification in the long-run injured no one but herself, besides putting her in the wrong, and giving Elizabeth a standing excuse for treating her as an enemy. England was permanently free from the menace of a disciplined French army in the northern kingdom. Nothing was settled in the treaty about religion. But this was equivalent to a confirmation of the violent change that had recently taken place; in itself a guarantee of security to England.

The moral effect of this success was even greater than its more tangible results. It had been very generally believed, at all events abroad, that Elizabeth was tottering on her throne; that the large majority were on the point of rising to depose her; that, wriggle as she might, she would find she was a mere *protégée* of Philip, with no option but to follow his directions and square her policy to his. Whatever small basis of fact underlay this delusive estimate had been ridiculously exaggerated in the reports sent to Philip by his ambassador De Quadra, a man who evidently paid more attention to hole-and-corner tattle than to the broad forces of English politics.

All these imaginings were now proved to be vain. Elizabeth had shown that she could protect herself by her own strength and in her own way. She had civilly ignored Philip's advice, or rather his injunctions. She had thrown down the glove to France, and France had not taken it up. She had placed in command of her armies the very man whom she was supposed to fear, and he had done her bidding, and done it well. England once more stood before Europe as an independent power, able to take care of itself, aid its friends, and annoy its enemies.

It is true that, as far as Elizabeth personally is concerned, her Scotch policy had not always in its execution been as prompt and firm as could be desired. Those who follow it in greater detail than is possible here will find much in it that is irresolute and even vacillating. This defect appears throughout Elizabeth's career, though it will always be ignored, as it ought to be ignored, by those who reserve their attention for what is worth observing in the course of human affairs.

In her intellectual grasp of European politics as a whole, and of the interests of her own kingdom, Elizabeth was probably superior to any of her counsellors.

No one could better than she think out the general idea of a political campaign. But theoretical and practical qualifications are seldom, if ever, combined in equal excellence. Not only are the qualities themselves naturally opposed, but the constant exercise of either increases the disparity. Her sex obliged Elizabeth to leave the large field of execution to others. Her practical gifts therefore, whatever they were, deteriorated rather than advanced as she grew older. In men, who every day and every hour of the day are engaged in action, the habit of prompt decision and persistence in a course once adopted, even if it be not quite the best, is naturally formed and strengthened. It is a habit so valuable, so indispensable to continued success, that in practice it largely compensates for some inferiority in conception and design. Elizabeth's irresolution and vacillation were therefore a consequence of her position—that of an extremely able and well-informed woman called upon to conduct a government in which so much had to be decided by the sovereign at her own discretion. The abler she was, the more disposed to make her will felt, the less steadiness and consistency in action were to be expected from her. As the wife of a king, upon whom the final responsibility would have rested—her inferior perhaps in intellect and knowledge, but with the masculine habit of making up his mind once for all, and then steering a straight course—she would have been a wise and enlightened adviser, not afraid of consistently maintaining principles, when the time, mode, and degree of their application rested with another. As it was, Cecil and other able statesmen who served her had not only to take their general course of policy from their mistress—a wise course upon the whole, wiser sometimes than they would have selected for themselves—but they were embarrassed, in their loyal attempts to steer in the direction she had prescribed, by her nervous habit of catching at the rudder-lines whenever a new doubt occurred to her ingenious mind, or some private feeling of the woman perverted the clear insight of the sovereign.

The rivalry between France and Spain had hitherto been the safety of England. Nothing but reasons of religion could bring those two powers to suspend their political quarrel. This danger seemed to be averted for the moment by the temporary ascendant of the Politiques after the death of Francis II. But the fanaticism of both Catholics and Huguenots was too bitter, and the nobles on both sides were too ambitious, to listen to the dictates of reason and patriotism. The immense majority of the nation, except in some districts of the south and south-west, was profoundly Catholic. The Huguenots, strongest amongst the aristocracy and the upper bourgeoisie, daring and intolerant like the Calvinists everywhere, had no sooner received some countenance from Catherine than they began to preach against the mass, to demand the spoliation of the Church, the suppression of monasteries, the destruction of images, and the expulsion of the Guises. Where they were strong enough they began to carry out their programme. The Guises, on the other hand, forgetting the glory they had won in the wars against Spain, were soliciting the patronage of Philip, and urging him to put himself at the head of a crusade against the heretics of all countries. To this appeal he replied by formally summoning Catherine to put down heresy in France. An accidential collision at Vassy, in which a number of Huguenots were slain, brought on the first of those wars of religion which were to desolate France for the next thirty years (March 1562). Both factions, equally dead to patriotism, opened their country to foreigners. The Guises called in the forces of Spain and the Pope. Condé applied to Elizabeth and the Protestant princes of Germany.

It was necessary to give the Huguenots just so much help as would prevent them from being crushed. Aggressive in appearance, such interference was in reality legitimate self-defence. But unfortunately neither Elizabeth nor her Council had forgotten Calais, and they extorted from Condé the surrender of Havre as a pledge for its restoration. In the case of Scotland they had come, as we have seen, to recognise that to establish a permanent raw by holding fortified posts on the territory of another nation is poor statesmanship. The possession of Calais was of little military value as against France. It is true that it would enable England to make sea communication between Spain and the Netherlands very insecure, and would thus give Philip a powerful motive for desiring to stand well with this country. But such a calculation had less weight with Englishmen at that moment than pure Jingoism—the longing to be again able to crow over their French enemy.

The occupation of Havre (October 1562) gave to the Huguenot cause the minimum of assistance, and brought upon it the maximum of odium. A hollow reconciliation was soon patched up between the rival factions (March 1563), and Elizabeth was summoned to evacuate Havre. She refused, loudly complaining of the Huguenots for deserting her. She "had come to the quiet possession of Havre without force or any other unlawful means, and she had good reason to keep it." Up to this time the fiction of peace between the two nations had been maintained. It was now open war. It is only fair to Elizabeth to say that all her Council and the whole nation were even hotter than she was. The garrison of Havre, with their commander Warwick, were eager for the fray. They would "make the French cock cry Cuck," they would "spend the last drop of their blood before the French should fasten a foot in the town." The inhabitants were all expelled, and the siege began, Condé as well as the Catholics appearing in the Queen-mother's army. After a valiant defence the English, reduced to a handful of men by typhus, sailed away (July 28, 1563). Peace was concluded early in the next year (April 1564). Elizabeth did not repeat her mistake. Thenceforward to the end of her reign we shall find her carefully cultivating friendly relations with every ruler of France.

CHAPTER IV

ELIZABETH AND MARY STUART: 1559-1568

WHEN Elizabeth mounted the throne, it was taken for granted that she was to marry, and marry with the least possible delay. This was expected of her, not merely because in the event of her dying without issue there would be a dispute whether the claim of Mary Stuart or that of Catherine Grey was to prevail, but for a more general reason. The rule of an unmarried woman, except provisionally during such short interval as might be necessary to provide her with a husband, was regarded as quite out of the question. It was the custom for the husbands of heiresses to step into the property of their wives and stand in the shoes, so to speak, of the last male proprietor, in order to perform those duties which could not be efficiently performed by a woman. Elizabeth's sister, while a subject, had no thought of marrying. But her accession was considered by herself and every one else to involve marriage. If the nobles of England could have foreseen that Elizabeth would elude this obligation, she would probably never have been allowed to mount the throne. Her marriage was thought to be as much a matter of course, and as necessary, as her coronation.

Accordingly the House of Commons, which met a month after her accession, immediately requested her to select a husband without delay. Her declaration that she had no desire to change her state was supposed to indicate only the real or affected coyness to be expected from a young lady. There was no lack of suitors, foreign or English. The Archduke Charles, son of the Emperor and cousin of Philip, would have been welcomed by all Catholics and acquiesced in by political Protestants like Cecil. The ardent Protestants were eager for Arran, and Cecil, till he saw it was useless, worked his best for him, regardless of the personal sacrifice his mistress must make in wedding a man who was not always quite sane and eventually became a confirmed lunatic.

Not many months of the new reign had passed before it began to be suspected that Elizabeth's partiality for Lord Robert Dudley had something to do with her evident distaste for all her suitors. To her Ministers and the public this partiality for a married man became a cause of great disquietude. They not unnaturally feared that with a young woman who had no relations to advise and keep watch over her, it might lead to some disastrous scandal incompatible with her continuance on the throne. Marriage with Dudley at this time was out of the question. But within four months of her accession, the Spanish ambassador mentions a report that Dudley's wife had a cancer, and that the Queen was only waiting for her death to marry him.

About the humble extraction of Elizabeth's favourite much nonsense was talked in his lifetime by his ill-wishers, and has been duly repeated since. He was as well born as most of the peerage of that time; very few of whom could show nobility of any antiquity in the male line. The Duke of Norfolk being the only Duke at Elizabeth's accession, and in possession of an ancient title, was looked on as the head of his order. Yet it was only seventy-five years since a Howard had first reached the peerage in consequence of having had the good fortune to marry the heiress of the Mowbrays. Edmund Dudley, Minister of Henry VII. and father of Northumberland, was grandson of John, fourth Lord Dudley; and Northumberland, by his mother's side, was sole heir and representative of the ancient barony of De L'Isle, which title he bore before he received his earldom and dukedom. In point of wealth and influence, indeed, the favourite might be called an upstart. The younger son of an attainted father, he had not an acre of land or a farthing of money which he did not owe either to his wife or to the generosity of Elizabeth. This it was that moved the sneers and ill-will of a people with whom nobility has always been a composite idea implying, not only birth and title, but territorial wealth. Moreover his grandfather, though of good extraction, was a simple esquire, and had risen by helping Henry VII. to trample on the old nobility. After his fall his son had climbed to power under Henry VIII. and Edward VI. in the same way. Lord Robert Dudley, again, had to begin at the bottom of the ladder.

No one will claim for Elizabeth's favourite that he was a man of distinguished ability or high character. He had a fine figure and a handsome face. He bore himself well in manly exercises. His manners were attractive when he wished to please. To these qualities he first owed his favour with Elizabeth, who was never at any pains to conceal her liking for good-looking men and her dislike of ugly ones. Finding himself in favour, and inheriting to the full the pushing audacity of his father and grandfather, he professed for the Queen a love which he certainly did not feel, in order to serve his soaring ambition. Elizabeth, it is my firm conviction, never loved Dudley or any other man, in any sense of the word, high or low. She had neither a tender heart nor a sensual temperament. But she had a more than feminine appetite for admiration; and the more she was, unhappily for herself, a stranger to the emotion of love, the more restlessly did she desire to be thought capable of inspiring it. She was therefore easily taken in by Dudley's professions, and, though she did not care for him enough to marry him, she liked to have him as well as several other handsome men, dangling about her, "like her lap-dog," to use her own expression. Further she believed—and here came in the mischief —that his devotion to her person would make him a specially faithful servant.

We know, though Elizabeth did not, that in 1561, Dudley was promising the Spanish ambassador to be Philip's humble vassal, and to do his best for Catholicism, if Philip would promote his marriage with the Queen; that, in the same year, he was offering his services to the French Huguenots for the same consideration; that at one time he posed as the protector of the Puritans, while at another he was intriguing with the captive Queen of Scots; whom, again, later on, he had a chief share in bringing to the block. But we must remember that very few statesmen, English or foreign, in the sixteenth century could have shown a record free from similar blots. Those who, like Elizabeth and Cecil, were undeniably actuated on the whole by public spirit, or by any principle more respectable than pure selfishness, never hesitated to lie or play a double game when it seemed to serve their turn. William of Orange is the only eminent statesman, as far as I know, against whom this charge cannot be made. When this was the standard of honour for consistent politicians and real patriots, what was to be expected of lower natures? Dudley's conduct on several occasions was bad and contemptible; and he must be judged with the more severity, because he sinned not only against the code of duty binding on the ordinary man and citizen, but against his professions of a tender sentiment by means of which he had acquired his special influence. I have said that he was not a man of great ability. But neither was he the empty-headed incapable trifler that some writers have depicted him. He was not so judged by his contemporaries. That Elizabeth, because she liked him, would have selected a man of notorious incapacity to command her armies, both in the Netherlands and when the Armada was expected, is one of those hypotheses that do not become more credible by being often repeated. Cecil himself, when it was not a question of the marriage—of which he was a determined opponent—regarded him as a useful servant of the Queen. I do not doubt that Elizabeth estimated his capacity at about its right value. What she over-estimated was his affection for herself, and consequently his trustworthiness. Sovereigns—and others—often place a near relative in an important post, not as being the most capable person they know, but as most likely to be true to them. Elizabeth had no near relatives. If we grant—as we must grant—that she believed in Dudley's love, we cannot wonder that she employed him in positions of trust. A female ruler will always be liable to make these mistakes, unless her Ministers and captains are to be of her own sex.

On the 3rd of September 1560, two months after the Treaty of Leith, Elizabeth told De Quadra that she had made up her mind to marry the Archduke Charles. On the 8th, Lady Robert Dudley died at Cumnor Hall. On the 11th, Elizabeth told De Quadra that she had changed her mind. Dudley neglected his wife, and never brought her to court. We cannot doubt that he fretted under a tie which stood in the way of his ambition. Her death had been predicted. It is not strange, therefore, that he should have been suspected of having caused it. Nevertheless, not a particle of evidence pointing in that direction has ever been produced, and it seems most probable that the poor deserted creature committed suicide. A coroner's jury investigated the case diligently, and, it would seem, with some animus against Foster, the owner of Cumnor Hall, but returned a verdict of accidental death.

Anyhow, Dudley was now free. The Scotch Estates were eagerly pressing Arran's suit, and the English Protestants were as eagerly backing them. The opportunity was certainly unique. Though nothing was said about deposing Mary, yet nothing could be more certain than that, if this marriage took place, the Queen of France would never reign in Scotland.

At her wits' end how to escape a match so desirable for the Queen, so repulsive to the woman, Elizabeth had announced her willingness to espouse the Archduke in order to gain a short breathing-time. Vienna was at least further than Edinburgh, and difficulties were sure to arise when details began to be discussed. At this moment, by the sudden death of his wife, Dudley became marriageable. If Elizabeth had been free to marry or not, as she pleased, it seems to me in the highest degree improbable that she would ever have thought of taking Dudley. But believing that a husband was inevitable, and expecting that she would be forced to take some one who was either unknown to her or positively distasteful, it was most natural that she should ask herself whether it was not the least of evils to put this cruel persecution to an end by choosing a man whom at least she admired and liked, who loved her, as she thought, for her own sake, and would be as obedient " as her lap-dog." When nations are ruled by women, and marriageable women, feelings and motives which belong to the sphere of private life, and should be confined to it, are apt to invade the domain of politics. If Elizabeth's subjects expected their sovereign to suppress all personal feelings in choosing a consort, they ought to have established the Salic law. No woman, queen or not queen, can be expected voluntarily to make such a sacrifice. Her happiness is too deeply involved.

In the autumn, then, of 1560, when Elizabeth had been not quite two years on the throne, she seriously thought of marrying Dudley. It is difficult to say how long she continued to think of it seriously. With him, as with other suitors, she went on coquetting when she had perfectly made up her mind that nothing was to come of it. Perhaps we shall be right in saying that, as long as there was any question of the Archduke Charles, she looked to Dudley as a possible refuge. This would be till about the beginning of 1568. It seems to be always assumed, as a matter of course, that Cecil played the part of Elizabeth's good genius in persistently dissuading her from marrying Dudley. I am not so sure of this. If she had been a wife and a mother many of her difficulties would have at once disappeared, and the weakest points in her character would have no longer been brought out. It ended in her not marrying at all. I am inclined to think that another enemy of Dudley, the Earl of Sussex, showed more good sense and truer patriotism when he wrote in October 1560:—

"I wish not her Majesty to linger this matter of so great importance, but to choose speedily; and therein to follow so much her own affection as [that], by the looking upon him whom she should choose, *omnes ejus sensus titillarentur*; which shall be the readiest way, with the help of God, to bring us a blessed prince which shall redeem us out of thraldom. If I knew that England had other rightful inheritors I would then advise otherwise, and seek to serve the time by a husband's choice [seek for an advantageous political alliance]. But seeing that she is *ultimum refugium*, and that no riches, friendship, foreign alliance, or any other present commodity that might come by a husband, can serve our turn, without issue of her body, if the Queen will love anybody, let her love where and whom she lists, so much thirst I to see her love. And whomsoever she shall love and choose, him will I love, honour, and serve to the uttermost."

Perhaps I may be excused for expressing the opinion that the ideal husband for Elizabeth, if it had been possible, would have been Lord James Stuart, afterwards Earl of Moray. Of sufficient capacity, kindly heart, undaunted resolution, and unswerving rectitude of purpose, he would have supplied just those elements that were wanting to correct her defects. King of Scotland he perhaps could not be. Regent of Scotland he did become. If he could, at the same time, have been Elizabeth's husband, the two crowns might have, in the next generation, been worn by a Stuart of a nobler stock than the son of Mary and Darnley.

When Mary Stuart, on the death of her husband Francis II., returned to her own kingdom (August 1561), she found the Scotch nobles sore at the rejection of Arran's suit. Bent on giving a sovereign to England, in one way or another, they were now ready, Protestants as well as Catholics, to back Mary's demand that she should be recognised as Elizabeth's heir-presumptive. To this the English Queen could not consent, for the very sufficient reason, that not only would the Catholic party be encouraged to hold together and give trouble, but the more bigoted and desperate members of it would certainly attempt her life, lest she should disappoint Mary's hopes by marrying. "She was not so foolish," she said, "as to hang a winding-sheet before her eyes or make a funeral feast whilst she was alive," but she promised that she would neither do anything nor allow anything to be done by Parliament to prejudice Mary's title. To this undertaking she adhered long after Mary's hostile conduct had given ample justification for treating her as an enemy.

Openly Mary was claiming nothing but the succession. In reality she cared little for a prospect so remote and uncertain. What she was scheming for was to hurl Elizabeth from her throne. This was an object for which she never ceased to work till her head was off her shoulders. Her aims were more sharply defined than those of Elizabeth, and she was remarkably free from that indecision which too often marred the action of the English Queen. In ability and information she was not at all inferior to Elizabeth; in promptitude and energy she was her superior. These masculine qualities might have given her the victory in the bitter duel, but that, in the all-important domain of feeling, her sex indomitably asserted itself, and weighted her too heavily to match the superb self-control of Elizabeth. She could love and she could hate; Elizabeth had only likes and dislikes, and therefore played the cooler game. When Mary really loved, which was only once, all selfish calculations were flung to the winds; she was ready to sacrifice everything, and not count the cost—body and soul, crown and life, interest and honour. When she hated, which was often, rancour was apt to get the better of prudence. And so at the fatal turning-point of her career, when mad hate and madder love possessed her soul, she went down before her great rival never to rise again. Here was a woman indeed. And if, for that reason, she lost the battle in life, for that reason too she still disputes it from the tomb. She has always had, and always will have, the ardent sympathy of a host of champions, to whom the "fair vestal throned by the west" is a mere politician, sexless, cold-blooded, and repulsive.

In 1564 Mary, as yet fancy-free, was seeking to match herself on purely political grounds. She was not so fastidious as Elizabeth, for she does not seem to have troubled herself at all about personal qualities, if a match seemed otherwise eligible. The Hamiltons pressed Arran upon her. But he was a Protestant. He was not heir to any throne but that of Scotland; and, though a powerful family in Scotland, the Hamiltons could give her no help elsewhere. Philip, who, now that the Guises had become his *protégés*, was less jealous of her designs, wished her to marry his cousin, the Archduke Charles of Austria. But this prince, whom Elizabeth professed to find too much of a Catholic, was, in the eyes of Mary and her more bigoted co-religionists, too nearly a Lutheran; and she doubted whether Philip cared enough for him to risk a war for establishing him and herself upon the English throne. For this reason the husband on whom she had set her heart was Don Carlos, Philip's own son, a sort of wild beast. But Philip received her overtures doubtfully; the fact being that he could not trust Don Carlos, whom he eventually put to death. Catherine de' Medici loved Mary as little as she did the other Guises, but the prospect of the Spanish match filled her with such terror that she proposed to make the Scottish Queen her daughter-in-law a second time by a marriage with Charles IX., a lad under thirteen, if she would wait two years for him.

On the other hand, Elizabeth impressed upon Mary

that, unless she married a member of some Reformed Church, the English Parliament would certainly demand that her title to the succession, whatever it was, should be declared invalid. The House of Commons was strongly Protestant, and had with difficulty been prevented from addressing the Queen in favour of the succession of Lady Catherine Grey. Apart from religion there was deep irritation against the whole Scotch nation. Sir Ralph Sadler, who had been much employed in Scotland, denounced them as "false, beggarly, and perjured, whom the very stones in the English streets would rise against." When Elizabeth was dangerously ill in October 1562, the Council discussed whom they should proclaim in the event of her death. Some were for the will of Henry VIII. and Catherine Grey. Others, sick of female rulers, were for taking the Earl of Huntingdon, a descendant of the Duke of Clarence. None were for Mary or Darnley. Mary's chief friends—Montagu, Northumberland, Westmoreland, and Derby—were not on the Council.

Parliament and the Council being against her, Mary could not afford to quarrel with the Queen. Elizabeth told her that she would regard a marriage with any Spanish, Austrian, or French prince as a declaration of war. Help from those quarters was far away, and at the mercy of winds and waves: the Border fortresses were near, and their garrisons always ready to march. Besides, whichever of the two she might obtain—Charles IX. or the Archduke—she drove the other into the arms of Elizabeth.

But there was another possible husband who had crossed her mind from time to time; not a prince indeed, yet of royal extraction in the female line, and, what was more, not without pretensions to that very succession which she coveted. Henry Lord Darnley, son of Matthew Stuart, Earl of Lennox, was, by his father's side, of the royal family of Scotland, while his mother was the daughter of Margaret Tudor, sister of Henry VIII., by her second husband, the Earl of Angus. Born and brought up in England, where his father had been long an exile, he was reckoned as an Englishman, which, in the opinion of many lawyers, was essential as a qualification for the crown. He was also a Catholic, and if Elizabeth had died at this time, it was perhaps Darnley, rather than Mary, whom the Catholics would have tried to place on the throne. Elizabeth had promised that, if Mary would marry an English nobleman, she would do her best to get Mary's title recognised by Parliament. To Elizabeth, therefore, Mary now turned, with the request that she would point out such a nobleman, not without a hope that she would name Darnley (March 1564). But, to Mary's mortification, she formally recommended Lord Robert Dudley.

This recommendation has often been treated as if it was a sorry joke perpetrated by Elizabeth, who had never any intention of furthering, or even permitting, such a match. But nothing is more certain than that Elizabeth was most anxious to bring it about; and it affords a decisive proof that her feeling for Dudley, whatever name she herself may have put to it, was not what is usually called love. Cecil and all her most intimate advisers entertained no doubt that she was sincere. She undertook, if Mary would accept

Dudley, to make him a duke; and, in the meantime, she created him Earl of Leicester. She regarded him, so she told Mary's envoy Melville, as her brother and her friend; if he was Mary's husband she would have no suspicion or fear of any usurpation before her death, being assured that he was so loving and trusty that he would never permit anything to be attempted during her time. "But," she said, pointing to Darnley, who was present, "you like better yonder long lad." Her suspicion was correct. Melville had secret instructions to procure permission for Darnley to go to Scotland. However, he answered discreetly that "no woman of spirit could choose such an one who more resembled a woman than a man."

How was Elizabeth to be persuaded to let Darnley leave England? There was only one way to disarm suspicion: Mary declared herself ready to marry Leicester (January 1565). Darnley immediately obtained leave of absence for three months ostensibly to recover the forfeited Lennox' property. In Scotland the purpose of his coming was not mistaken, and it roused the Protestants to fury. The Queen's chapel, the only place in the Lowlands where mass was said, was beset. Her priests were mobbed and maltreated. Moray, who till lately had supported his sister with such loyalty and energy that Knox had quarrelled with him, prepared, with the other Lords of the Congregation, for resistance. Elizabeth, and Cecil also, had been completely overreached. A prudent player sometimes gets into difficulties by attributing equal prudence to a daring and reckless antagonist. Elizabeth, as a patriotic ruler, desired nothing but peace and security for her own kingdom. If she could have that, she had no wish to meddle with Scotland. Mary, caring nothing for the interests of her subjects, was facing civil war with a light heart; and, for the chance of obtaining the more brilliant throne, was ready to risk her own.

Undeterred by Elizabeth's threats, Mary married Darnley (July 29, 1565). Moray and Argyll, having obtained a promise of assistance from England, took arms; but most of the Lords of the Congregation showed themselves even more powerless or perfidious than they had been five years before. Morton, Ruthven, and Lindsay, stoutest of Protestants, were related to Darnley, and were gratified by the elevation of their kinsman. Moray failed to elicit a spark of spirit out of the priest-baiting citizens of Edinburgh, and the Queen, riding steel cap on head and pistols at saddle-bow, chased him into England. Lord Bedford, who was in command at Berwick, could have stepped across the Border and scattered her undisciplined array without difficulty. He implored Elizabeth to let him do it; offered to do it on his own responsibility, and be disavowed. But he found, to his mortification, that she had been playing a game of brag. She had hoped that a threatening attitude would stop the marriage. But as it was an accomplished fact, she was not going to draw the sword.

This was shabby treatment of Moray and his friends, and to some of her councillors it seemed not only shameful but dangerous to show the white feather. But judging from the course of events, Elizabeth's policy was the safe one. The English

Catholics—some of them at all events, as will be explained presently—were becoming more discontented and dangerous. The northern earls were known to be disaffected. Mary believed that in every country in England the Catholics had their organisation and their leaders, and that, if she chose, she could march to London. No doubt she was much deceived. In reluctance to resort to violence and respect for constituted authority, England, even north of the Humber, was at least two centuries ahead of Scotland, and, if she had come attended by a horde of savage Highlanders and Border ruffians, "the very stones in the streets would have risen against them." It was Elizabeth's rule—and a very good rule too—never to engage in a war if she could avoid it. From this rule she could not be drawn to swerve either by passion or ambition, or that most fertile source of fighting, a regard for honour. All the old objections to an invasion of Scotland still subsisted in full strength, and were reinforced by others. It was better to wait for an attack which might never come than go half-way to meet it. An invasion of Scotland might drive the northern earls to declare for Mary, which, unless compelled to choose sides, they might never do. Some people are more perturbed by the expectation and uncertainty of danger than by its declared presence. Not so Elizabeth. Smouldering treason she could take coolly as long as it only smouldered. As for the betrayal of the Scotch refugees, Elizabeth never allowed the private interests of her own subjects, much less those of foreigners, to weigh against the interests of England. Moray, one of the most magnanimous and self-sacrificing of statesmen, evidently felt that Elizabeth's course was wise, if not exactly chivalrous. He submitted to her public rebuke without publicly contradicting her, and waited patiently in exile till it should be convenient for her to help him and his cause. Mary, too, though elated by her success, and never abandoning her intention to push it further, found it best to halt for a while. Philip wrote to her that he would help her secretly with money if Elizabeth attacked her, but not otherwise, and warned her against any premature clutch at the English crown. Elizabeth's seeming tameness could hardly have received a more complete justification.

Mary had determined to espouse Darnley, before she had set eyes on him, for purely political reasons. There is no reason to suppose she ever cared for him. It is more likely, as Mr. Froude suggests, that for a great political purpose she was doing an act which in itself she loathed. A woman of twenty-two, already a widow, mature beyond her years, exceptionally able, absorbed in the great game of politics, and accustomed to admiration, was not likely to care for a raw lad of nineteen, foolish, ignorant, ill-conditioned, vicious, and without a single manly quality. One man we know she did love later on—loved passionately and devotedly, no slim girl-faced youngster, but the fierce, stout-limbed, dare-devil Bothwell; and Bothwell gradually made his way to her heart by his readiness to undertake every desperate service she required of him. What Mary admired, nay envied, in the other sex was the stout heart and the strong arm. She loved herself to rough it on the war-path. She surprised Randolph by her spirit:—"Never thought I that stomach to be in her that I find. She repented nothing but, when the Lords and others came in the morning from the watches, that she was not a man, to know what life it was to lie all night in the fields or to walk upon the causeway with a jack and a knapscap, a Glasgow buckler and a broadsword." "She desires much," says Knollys, "to hear of hardiness and valiancy, commending by name all approved hardy men of her country, although they be her enemies; and she concealeth no cowardice even in her friends." Valuable to Mary as a man of action, Bothwell was not worth much as an adviser. For advice she looked to the Italian Rizzio, in whom she confided because, with the detachment of a foreigner, he regarded Scotch ambitions, animosities, and intrigues only as so much material to be utilised for the purpose of the combined onslaught on Protestantism which the Pope was trying to organise. Bothwell was at this time thirty, and Rizzio, according to Lesley, fifty.

In spite of all the prurient suggestions of writers who have fastened on the story of Mary's life as on a savoury morsel, there is no reason whatever for thinking that she was a woman of a licentious disposition, and there is strong evidence to the contrary. There was never anything to her discredit in France. Her behaviour in the affair of Chastelard was irreproachable. The charge of adultery with Rizzio is dismissed as unworthy of belief even by Mr. Froude, the severest of her judges. Bothwell indeed she loved, and, like many another woman who does not deserve to be called licentious, she sacrificed her reputation to the man she loved. But the most conclusive proof that she was no slave to appetite is afforded by her nineteen years' residence in England, which began when she was only twenty-five. During almost the whole of that time she was mixing freely in the society of the other sex, with the fullest opportunity for misconduct had she been so inclined. It is not to be supposed that she was fettered by any scruples of religion or morality. Yet no charge of unchastity is made against her.

When Darnley found that his wife, though she conferred on him the title of King, did not procure for him the crown matrimonial or allow him the smallest authority, he gave free vent to his anger. No less angry were his kinsmen, Morton, Ruthven, and Lindsay. They had deserted the Congregation in the expectation that when Darnley was King they would be all-powerful. Instead of this they found themselves neglected; while the Queen's confidence was given to Catholics and to Bothwell, who, though nominally a Protestant, always acted with the Catholics. The Protestant seceders had in fact fallen between two stools. It was against Rizzio that their rage burnt fiercest. Bothwell was only a bull-headed, blundering swordsman. Rizzio was doubly detestable to them as the brain of the Queen's clique and as a low-born foreigner. Rizzio, therefore, they determined to remove in the time-honoured Scottish fashion. Notice of the day fixed for the murder was sent to the banished noblemen in England, so that they might appear in Edinburgh immediately it was accomplished.

Randolph, the English ambassador, and Bedford, who commanded on the Border, were also taken into the secret, and they communicated it to Cecil and Leicester.

It is unnecessary here to repeat the well-known story of the murder of Rizzio. It was part of a large scheme for bringing back the exiled Protestant lords, closing the split in the Protestant party, and securing the ascendancy of the Protestant religion. At first it appeared to have succeeded. Bedford wrote to Cecil that "everything would now go well." But Mary, by simulating a return of wifely fondness, managed to detach her weak husband from his confederates. By his aid she escaped from their hands. Bothwell and her Catholic friends gathered round her in arms. In a few days she re-entered Edinburgh in triumph, and Rizzio's murderers had to take refuge in England.

But if the Protestant stroke had failed, Mary was obliged to recognise that her plan for re-establishing the Catholic ascendancy in Scotland could not be rushed in the high-handed way she had proposed as a mere preliminary to the more important subjugation of England. At the very moment when she seemed to stand victorious over all opposition, the ground had yawned under her feet, and, while she was dreaming of dethroning Elizabeth, she had found herself a helpless captive in the hands of her own subjects. The lesson was a valuable one, and if she could profit by it her prospects had never been so good. The barbarous outrage of which, in the sixth month of pregnancy, she had been the object could not but arouse wide-spread sympathy for her. She had extricated herself from her difficulties with splendid courage and cleverness. The loss of such an adviser as Rizzio was really a stroke of luck for her. All she had to do was to abandon, or at all events postpone, her design of re-establishing the Catholic religion in Scotland, and to discontinue her intrigues against Elizabeth.

Her prospects in England were still further improved when she gave birth to a son (June 19, 1566). Once more there was an heir-male to the old royal line, and, as Elizabeth continued to evade marriage, most people who were not fierce Protestants began to think it would be more reasonable and safe to abide by the rule of primogeniture than by the will of Henry VIII., sanctioned though it was by Act of Parliament. There can be no doubt that this was the opinion and intention of Elizabeth, though she strongly objected to having anything settled during her own lifetime. But she had herself gone a long way towards settling it by her treatment of Mary's only serious competitor. Catherine Grey had contracted a secret marriage with the Earl of Hertford, son of the Protector Somerset. Her pregnancy necessitated an avowal. The clergyman who had married them was not forthcoming, and Hertford's sister, the only witness, was dead. Elizabeth chose to disbelieve their story, though she would not have been able to prove when, where, or by whom her own father and mother had been married. She had a right to be angry; but when she sent the unhappy couple to the Tower, and caused her tool, Archbishop Parker, to pronounce the union invalid and its offspring illegitimate, she was playing Mary's game. The House of Commons elected in 1563 was still undissolved. It was strongly Protestant, and it favoured Catherine's title even after her disgrace. In its second session, in the autumn of 1566, it made a determined effort to compel Elizabeth to marry, and in the meanwhile to recognise Catherine as the heir-presumptive. The zealous Protestants knew well that the Peers were in favour of the Stuart title, and they feared that a new House of Commons might agree with the Peers. To get rid of their pertinacity Elizabeth dissolved Parliament, not without strong expressions of displeasure (Jan. 2, 1567). Cecil himself earned the thanks of Mary for his attitude on this occasion. It cannot be doubted that he dreaded her succession; but he saw which way the tide was running, and he thought it prudent to swim with it.

It was at this moment that Mary flung away all her advantage, and entered on the fatal course which led to her ruin. Her loathing for Darnley, her fierce desire to avenge on him the insults and outrage she had suffered, left no room in heart or mind for considerations of policy. She would have been glad to obtain a divorce. But the Catholic Church does not grant divorce for misconduct after marriage. Some pretext must be found for alleging that the marriage was null from the beginning. This did not suit Mary. It would have made her son illegitimate, and would have placed her in exactly the position of Catherine Grey. A mere separation *a toro* would not have suited her any better, for it would not have enabled her to contract another marriage.

When Mary's reliance on Bothwell grew into attachment, when her attachment warmed into love, it is impossible to fix with any exactness. Her infatuation presented itself to him as a grand opening for his daring ambition. A notorious profligate, he loved her—if the word is to be so degraded—as much or as little as he had loved twenty other women. What, however, he desired in her case, was marriage. A more sensible man would have foreseen that marriage would mean certain ruin for himself and the Queen. But he was accustomed to despise all difficulties in his path, being intellectually incapable of measuring them, and believing in nothing but audacity and brute force. Husband of the Queen, why should he not be master of the kingdom? Why not King? When such an idea had once occurred to Bothwell, Darnley's expectancy of life would be much the same as that of a calf in the presence of the butcher.

The wretched victim had alienated all his friends among the nobility. Some owed him a deadly grudge for his treachery. Others had been offended by his insolence. To all he was an encumbrance and a nuisance. Several, therefore, of the leading personages were more or less engaged in the compact for putting him out of the way. Moray, Argyll, and Maitland offered to assist in ridding Mary of her husband by way of a Protestant sentence of divorce, on condition that Morton and his friends in exile should be pardoned and recalled. The bargain was struck, and Mary assented to it. Nothing was said about murder. No one had any interest in murder except Mary and Bothwell, whose project of marriage was as yet unsuspected. At the same time, if Bothwell liked to kill Darnley on his own responsibility, as no doubt he made it pretty plain that he would—why, so much the better. It relieved the other lords of all trouble. It was a simple, thorough, old-fashioned expedient, which had never been attended with any discredit in Scotland, and had only one inconvenience —that it usually saddled the murderer with a blood feud. In the present case Lennox was the only peer who would feel the least aggrieved; and he was in no condition to wage blood-feuds. Anyhow, that was Bothwell's look-out.

So obvious was all this that it was hardly worth while to observe secrecy except as to the exact occasion and mode of execution. Many persons were more or less aware of what was going to be done; but none cared to interfere. Moray was an honourable and conscientious man, if judged by the standard of his environment—the only fair way of estimating character. But Moray chose to leave Edinburgh the morning before the deed; and thought it sufficient to be able to say afterwards that "if any man said he was present when purposes [talk] were held in his audience tending to any unlawful or dishonourable end, he spoke wickedly and untruly." The inner circle of the plot consisted of Bothwell, Argyll, Huntly, Maitland, and Sir James Balfour.

That Darnley was murdered by Bothwell is not disputed. That Mary was cognisant of the plot, and lured him to the shambles, has been doubted by few investigators at once competent and unbiassed. She lent herself to this part not without compunction. Bothwell had the advantage over her that the loved has over the lover; and he used it mercilessly for his headlong ambition, hardly taking the trouble to pretend that he cared for the unhappy woman who was sacrificing everything for him. He in fact cared more for his lawful wife, whom he was preparing to divorce, and to whom he had been married only six months. Mary was tormented by jealousy of her after the divorce as well as before.

The murder of Darnley (Feb. 10, 1567) was universally ascribed to Mary at the time by Catholics as well as Protestants at home and abroad, and it fatally damaged her cause in England and the rest of Europe. In Scotland itself—such was the backward and barbarous state of the country—it would probably not have shaken her throne if she had followed it up with firm and prudent government. She might even have indulged her illicit passion for Bothwell, with little pretence of concealment, if she had not advanced him in place and power above his equals. There was probably not a noble in Scotland, from Moray downwards, who would have scrupled to be her Minister. The Protestant commonalty indeed, who with all the national laxity as to the observance of the sixth commandment, were shocked by any trifling with the seventh, would no doubt have made their bark heard. But their bite had not yet become formidable; and in any case they were not to be propitiated.

What brought sudden and irretrievable ruin on Mary was not the murder of Darnley, but the infatuation which made her the passive instrument of Bothwell's presumptuous ambition. The lords, Catholic and Protestant alike, allowed the murder to pass uncondemned and unpunished; but they were furious when they found that Darnley had only been removed to make room for Bothwell, and that they were to have for their master a noble of by no means the highest lineage, bankrupt in fortune, and generally disliked for his arrogant and bullying demeanour. The project of marriage was not disclosed till ten weeks after the murder (April 19, 1567). Five days later, Bothwell, fearing lest he should be frustrated by public indignation or interference from England, carried off the Queen, as had been previously arranged between them. His idea was that, when Mary had been thus publicly outraged, it would be recognised as impossible that she should marry any one but the ravisher. In this coarse expedient, as in the clumsy means employed for disposing of Darnley, we see the blundering foolhardiness of the man. The marriage ceremony was performed as soon as Bothwell's divorce could be managed (May 15). Just a month later Mary surrendered to the insurgent lords at Carberry Hill, and Bothwell, flying for his life, disappears from history.

The feelings with which Elizabeth had contemplated the course of events in Scotland during the last six months were no doubt of a mixed nature. At the beginning of 1567, her seven-years' duel with Mary appeared to be ending · in defeat. The last bold thrust, aimed in her interest if not by her hand —the murder of Rizzio—had not improved her position. It seemed that she would soon be obliged to make her choice between two equally dreaded alternatives: she must either recognise Mary as her heir or take a husband. From this unpleasant dilemma she was released by the headlong descent of her rival in the first six months of 1567. But all other feelings were soon swallowed up in alarm and indignation at the spectacle of subjects in revolt against their sovereign. As tidings came in rapid succession of Mary's surrender at Carberry Hill, of her return to Edinburgh amidst the insults and threats of the Calvinist mob, of her imprisonment at Loch Leven, of the proposal to try and execute her, Elizabeth's anger waxed hotter, and she told the Scotch lords in her most imperious tones that she could not, and would not, permit them to use force with their sovereign. If they deposed or punished her, she would revenge it upon them. If they could not prevail on her to do what was right, they must "remit themselves to Almighty God, in whose hands only princes' hearts remain."

This language, addressed as it was to the only men in Scotland who were disposed to support the English interest, was imprudent. In her fellow-feeling for a sister sovereign, and her keen perception of the revolutionary tendencies of the time, Elizabeth spoilt an unique opportunity of placing her relations with Scotland on a footing of permanent security, of providing for the English succession in a way at once advantageous to the nation and free from risk to her own life, and lastly, of escaping from the constant worry about her own marriage. She had seen clearly enough what might be made of the situation. Throgmorton had been despatched to Scotland with instructions to do his best to get the infant Prince confided to her care. Once in England, she would virtually have adopted him. She would have possessed a son and heir without the inconvenience of marriage. To a Parliamentary recognition, indeed, of his title she would assuredly not have consented. It would have made him independent and dangerous. But if he behaved well to her, his succession would be more certain than any Act of Parliament could make it. Mary, if released and restored to power, would no longer be formidable. If she were deposed or put to death, Elizabeth would indirectly govern Scotland, at all events, till James should be of age.

This splendid opportunity Elizabeth lost by her peremptory and domineering language. The old Scotch pride took fire. The Anglophile lords, who would have been glad enough to send the young Prince to England, could not afford to appear less patriotic than the Francophiles. Throgmorton's attempt to get hold of James was as unsuccessful as that of the Protector Somerset to get hold of James's mother had been twenty years before. He was told that, before the Prince could be sent to England, his title to the English succession must be recognised; a condition which Elizabeth could not grant. Her claim that Mary should be restored without conditions was equally unacceptable to the Anglophile lords. They might have been induced to release her if she would have consented to give up Bothwell, or if they could have caught and hanged him. But such was her devotion to him, that no threats or promises availed to shake it. It was in vain that they offered to produce letters of his to the divorced Lady Bothwell, in which he assured her that he regarded her still as

E

his lawful wife, and Mary only as his concubine. The unhappy Queen had been aware even before her marriage — as a pathetic letter to Bothwell shows—that her passionate love was not returned. Two days after the marriage, his unkindness had driven her to think of suicide. But nothing they could say could shake her constancy. "She would not consent by any persuasion to abandon the Lord Bothwell for her husband. She would live and die with him. If it were put to her choice to relinquish her crown and kingdom or the Lord Bothwell, she would leave her kingdom and dignity to go as a simple damsel with him; and she will never consent that he shall fare worse or have more harm than herself. Let them put Bothwell and herself on board ship to go wherever fortune might carry them." This temper made it difficult for the Anglophile lords to know what to do with the prisoner of Loch Leven. They were disappointed and angry that Elizabeth, instead of approving their enterprise, and sending the money for which, as usual, they were begging, should treat them as rebels, and even secretly urge the Hamiltons to rescue Mary by force. The Hamiltons were in arms at Dumbarton. They wanted either that the Prince should be proclaimed King, with the Duke of Chatelherault for Regent, or that Mary should be divorced from Bothwell and married to Lord John Hamilton, the Duke's second son, and, in default of the crazy Arran, his destined successor. With Argyll, too, disgust at Mary's crime was tempered by a desire to marry her to his brother. Lady Douglas of Loch Leven herself, for whom Sir Walter Scott has invented such magnificent tirades, desired nothing better than to be her mother-in-law.

The prompt action of the confederate lords foiled these schemes. By the threat of a public trial on the charge of complicity in her husband's murder, or, as her advocates believe, by the fear of instant death, Mary was compelled to abdicate in favour of her son, and to nominate Moray Regent (July 29, 1567). Elizabeth would not recognise him; partly from a natural fear lest she should be suspected of having been in collusion with him all along, partly from genuine abhorrence of such revolutionary proceedings. The French Government, on the other hand, casting principle and sentiment alike to the winds, courted his alliance. He might keep his sister in prison, or put her to death, or send her to be immured in a French convent: only let him embrace the French interests, and an army should be sent to support him —a Huguenot army if he did not like Catholics. But Moray turned a deaf ear to these solicitations, and waited patiently till Elizabeth's ill-humour should give way to more statesmanlike considerations.

The escape of Mary from Loch Leven (May 2, 1568), and the rising of the Hamiltons in her favour, were largely due to the unfriendly attitude assumed by Elizabeth to the Regent's government. After the defeat of Langside (May 13) it would perhaps have been difficult for the fugitive Queen to make her way to France or Spain. But it was not the difficulty which deterred her from making the attempt. Both Catherine and Philip, later on, were disposed to befriend her, or, rather, to make use of her; but at the time of her escape from Scotland, she had nothing to expect from them but severity. Elizabeth was the only sovereign who had tried to help her. Moreover, Mary had always laboured under the delusion that because most Englishmen regarded her as the next heir to the crown, and a great many preferred the old religion to the new, she had as good a party in England as Elizabeth herself, if not a better. During her prosperity, she had made repeated applications to be allowed to visit the southern kingdom. She was convinced that, if she once appeared on English ground, Elizabeth's throne would be shaken; and Elizabeth's unwillingness to receive the visit had confirmed her in her belief. If she now crossed the Solway without waiting for the permission which she had requested by letter, it was not because she was hard pressed. The Regent had gone to Edinburgh after the battle. At Dundrennan, among the Catholic Maxwells, Lord Herries guaranteed her safety for forty days; and, at an hour's notice, a boat would place her beyond pursuit. Her haste was rather prompted by the expectation that Elizabeth, alarmed by her application, would refuse to receive her.

To Elizabeth the arrival of the Scottish Queen was, indeed, as unwelcome as it was unexpected. For ten years she had governed successfully, because she had managed to hold an even course between conflicting principles and parties, and to avoid taking up a decisive attitude on the most burning questions. The very indecision, which was the weak spot in her character, and which so fretted her Ministers, had, it must be confessed, contributed something to the result.

Cecil might groan over a policy of letting things drift. But it may be doubted whether they had not often drifted better than Cecil would have steered them if he might have had his way. To do nothing is not, indeed, the golden rule of statesmanship. But at that time, England's peculiar position between France and Spain, and between Calvinism and Catholicism, enabled her ruler to play a waiting game. This was the general rule applicable to the situation. Elizabeth apprehended it more clearly than her Ministers did, and she fell back on it again and again, when they flattered themselves that they had committed her to a forward policy. It was safe. It was cheap. It required coolness and intrepidity—qualities with which Elizabeth was well furnished by nature. But it was not spirited: it was not showy. Hence it has not found favour with historians, who insist that it ought to have ended in disaster. As a matter of fact, England was carried safely through unparalleled difficulties; and, when all is said, Elizabeth is entitled to be judged by the general result of her long reign.

Mary's arrival was unwelcome to Elizabeth, because it seemed likely to force her hand. To do nothing would be no longer possible. The Catholic nobles and gentry of the north flocked to Carlisle to pay court to the heiress of the English crown. It was not that they believed her innocent of her husband's murder. The suspicion of her complicity was at that time universal. But they supposed that it would never amount to more than a suspicion. They did not expect that the charge would ever be formally made. They were not aware that it could be supported by overwhelming evidence. Later on, when the proofs were produced, they had already committed themselves to her cause, and were bound not to be convinced.

If the attitude of these Catholics be thought to indicate some moral callousness, it may be fairly argued that it was less cynical than that of Elizabeth herself, who, while not unwilling that Mary should be suspected, would not allow her to be convicted. Steady to her main purpose, though hesitating, and even vacillating, in the means she adopted, she still adhered, notwithstanding all that had lately taken place, to her intention that Mary, if her survivor, should be her successor. Like all the greatest statesmen of her time, she placed secular interests before religious opinions. She was persuaded that the maintenance of the principle of authority was all-important. Nothing else could hold society together or prevent the rival fanaticisms from tearing each other to pieces. For authority there was no other basis left than the principle of hereditary succession by primogeniture. This principle must, therefore, be treated as something sacred—not to be set aside or tampered with in a short-sighted grasping at any seeming immediate utility. To allow it to be called in question was to shake her own title. Already, in France, the Jesuits were preaching that orthodoxy and the will of the people were the only legitimate foundation of sovereignty. Few English Catholics had learned that doctrine; but they would not be slow to learn it if the hereditary claim of Mary was to be set aside.

If Mary had been content to claim what primogeniture gave her—the right to the succession—there would have been no quarrel between her and Elizabeth. But it was notorious that she had all along been plotting to substitute herself for Elizabeth. Never had she cherished that dream with more confidence than when the Percys and Nevilles crowded round her at Carlisle. In her sanguine imagination, she already saw herself mistress of a finer kingdom than that which had just expelled her, and marching, at the head of her new subjects, to wreak vengeance on her old ones. She seemed likely to be no less dangerous as an exile in England than as a Queen in Scotland.

Elizabeth had now reason to regret the unnecessary warmth with which she had espoused Mary's cause. To suppose that she had any sentimental feelings for one whom she knew to be her deadly enemy is, in my judgment, ridiculous. Elizabeth was not a generous woman—especially towards other women; and in this case generosity would have been folly, and culpable folly. She did not hate Mary—she was too cool and self-reliant to hate an enemy—but she disliked her. She was jealous, with a small feminine jealousy, of her beauty and fascinations. The consciousness of this unworthy feeling made her all the more anxious not to betray it. And so, at a time when she did not expect to have Mary on her hands, she had been tempted to use language implying a pity, sympathy, and affection which assuredly she did not feel, and which it would not have been creditable to her to feel. Petty insincerities of this kind have usually to be paid for sooner or later. She had now to exchange the language of sympathy for the language of business with what grace she could; and she has not escaped the charge, certainly undeserved, of deliberate treachery. It was awkward, after such exaggerated professions of sympathy, to be obliged to hold the fugitive at arm's-length, and even to put restraint on her movements. But no other course was possible. No sovereign, at any time in history, has allowed a pretender to the crown to move about freely in his dominions and make a party among his subjects.

Wince as she might, and did, under the reproach of treachery, Elizabeth was not going to allow her unwise words to tie her to unwise action. Only one arrangement appeared to her to be at once admissible in principle and prudent in practice. Mary must be restored to the Scottish throne; but in such a way that she should thenceforth be powerless for mischief. She must be content with the title of Queen. The real government must· be in the hands of Moray. Thus the principle of legitimacy and the sacredness of royalty would be saved, and the English Catholics would be content to bide their time.

Cecil, for his part, was also anxious to see Mary back in Scotland; but not as Queen. Though regarded in Catholic circles as a desperate heretic, he was really a *politique*, a worldly-minded man—I mean the epithet to be laudatory—and he would probably have admitted in the abstract the wisdom of Elizabeth's opinion—that it was of more importance to England to have a legitimate sovereign than a gospel religion. But he was not prepared to submit frankly to the application of this principle. His personal prospects were too deeply concerned. It was all very well for Elizabeth to lay down a principle in which she might be said to have a life-interest. She was thirteen years his junior; but she might easily predecease him; and, with Mary on the throne, his power would certainly go, and, not improbably, his head with it. It was not in human nature, therefore, that he should cherish the principle of primogeniture as his mistress did; and, as far as his dread of her displeasure would allow him, he was always casting about for some means of defeating Mary's reversion. Her sudden plunge into crime was to him a turn of good fortune beyond his dreams. If he could have had his will she would have been promptly handed over to the Regent on the understanding that she was to be consigned to perpetual imprisonment, or, still better, to the scaffold.

In order to carry out her plan, Elizabeth called on Mary and the Regent to submit their respective cases to a Commission, consisting of the Duke of Norfolk, the Earl of Sussex, and Sir Ralph Sadler. Mary was extremely reluctant, as she well might be, to face any investigation; but she was told that, until her character was formally cleared, she could not be admitted to Elizabeth's presence; and she was at the same time privately assured that her restoration should, in any case, be managed without any damage to her honour. Moray received an equally positive assurance that if his sister was proved guilty, she should not be restored. The two statements were not absolutely irreconcilable, because Elizabeth intended to prevent the worst charges from being openly proved. Her sole object—and we can hardly blame her—was to obtain security for herself and her own kingdom. She did not wish the Queen of Scots to be proved a murderess in open court; but she did desire that the charge should be made, and also that the Commissioners should see the originals of the casket letters. Any public disclosure of the evidence might be prevented, and some sort of ambiguous acquittal pronounced, on grounds which all the world would see to be nugatory: such, for instance, as the culprit's own solemn denial of the charge; which was, in fact, the only answer Mary intended to make. What was known to the Commissioners would come to be more or less known to all persons of influence in England, and would surely discredit Mary to such a degree that even her warmest partisans would cease to conspire in her favour. Mary herself (so Elizabeth hoped), when made aware that this terrible weapon was in reserve, and could at any moment be used against her, would be permanently humbled and crippled, and would be glad to accept such terms as Elizabeth would impose.

The Commissioners opened their court at York (October 1568). But they had not been sitting long before Elizabeth discovered that Norfolk was scheming to marry Mary, and that the project was approved by many of the English nobility. Their purpose was not, as yet, disloyal. They thought that, married to the head of the English peerage, and residing in England, Mary would have to give up her plots with France, while her presence would strengthen the Conservative party, which desired to keep up the old alliance with Spain, and looked for the re-establishment sooner or later of the old religion. This scheme, though not disloyal, was extremely alarming to Elizabeth. Norfolk was nominally a Protestant. But she had placed him on the Commission as a representative of the Conservative party, believing that, while he would lend himself to hushing up Mary's guilt, his eyes would be opened to her real character. Yet here he was, like the Hamiltons, Campbells, and Douglases, ready to take her with her smirched reputation, simply for the chance of her two crowns. It was not a case of love, for he had never seen her. He seems to have been staggered for a moment by the sight of the casket letters, and to have doubted whether it was for his honour or even his safety to marry such a woman. But in the end, as we shall see, he swallowed his scruples.

On discovering Norfolk's intrigue, Elizabeth hastily revoked the Commission, and ordered another investigation to be held by the most important peers and statesmen of England. The casket letters and the depositions were submitted to them. Mary's able and zealous advocate, the Bishop of Ross, could say nothing except that his mistress had sent him on the supposition that Moray was to be the defendant: let her appear in person before the Queen, and she would give reasons why Moray ought not to be allowed to advance any charges against her. To make no better answer than this was virtually to admit that the charges against her were unanswerable.

It was thought that she was now sufficiently frightened to be ready to accept Elizabeth's terms, and they were unofficially communicated to her. Her return to Scotland was no longer contemplated, for Moray had absolutely declined to charge her openly with the murder or produce the letters unless she were detained in England. But in order to get rid of the revolutionary proceedings at Loch Leven she herself, as it were of her own free will, and on the ground that she was weary of government, was to confer the crown on her son and the regency on Moray. James was to be educated in England. She herself was to reside in England as long as Elizabeth should find it convenient. It was not mentioned in the communication, but it was probably intended, that she should marry some Englishman of no political importance, in order to produce more children who would succeed James if, as was likely enough, he should die in his infancy. If she would accept these conditions the charges against her should be "committed to perpetual silence;" if not, the trial must go on, and the verdict could not be doubtful (December 1568).

A woman less daring and less keen-sighted than Mary would assuredly, at this point, have given up the game, and thankfully accepted the conditions offered. They would not have prevented her from ascending the English throne if she had outlived Elizabeth. But that was a delay which she had always scouted as intolerable, and she was one to whom life was worth nothing if it meant defeat, retirement, even for a time, from the public scene, and the abandonment of long-cherished ambitions. Moreover her quick wit had divined that Elizabeth was using a threat which she did not mean to put into execution. There would be no verdict—not even any publication to the world of the evidence. Guilty therefore as she was, and aware that her guilt could be proved, she coolly faced "the great extremities" at which Elizabeth had hinted, and rejected the conditions.

Perhaps even Mary's daring would have flinched from this bold game but for a quarrel between Elizabeth and Philip, to be mentioned presently. Hitherto Philip, much to his credit, had declined to interfere in Mary's behalf. To him, as to every one else, Catholic as well as Protestant, her guilt seemed evident. She had been only a scandal and embarrassment to the Catholic cause. But if there was to be war with England, every enemy of Elizabeth was a weapon to be used. Accordingly he now began, though reluctantly, to think of helping the Queen of Scots, and even of marrying her to his brother Don John of Austria. With the prospect of such backing it was not wonderful that she declined to own herself beaten.

Elizabeth's calculations, though reasonable, were thus disappointed. The inquiry was dropped without any decision. The Regent was sent home with a small sum of money, and Mary remained in England (January 1569).

CHAPTER V

ARISTOCRATIC PLOTS : 1568-1572

FROM the beginning of the reign Cecil had never ceased to impress upon his mistress that a French or Spanish invasion on behalf of the Pope might at any time be expected, and that she should hurry to meet it by forming a league with the foreign Protestants of both Confessions, and vigorously assisting them to carry on a war of religion on the Continent. He was assuredly too well informed to believe that France and Spain would cease to counteract each other's designs on England, or that Lutherans and Calvinists would heartily combine for mutual defence. The enemies he really feared were his Catholic countrymen, with whom he would have to fight for his head if Elizabeth should die. He therefore desired to force on the struggle in her lifetime, when they would be rebels, and he would wield the power of the Crown.

Elizabeth, on the other hand, was against interference on the Continent, because it would be the surest way to bring upon England the calamity of invasion. She saw as plainly as Cecil did that it would compel her to throw herself into the arms of her own Protestants and to become, like her two predecessors, the mere chief of a party; whereas she meant to be the Queen of all Englishmen, and to tranquillise the natural fears of each party by letting it see that it would not be sacrificed to the violence of the other. Moreover the unbridled ascendancy of the Protestants would mean such alterations in the established worship as would have driven from the parish churches thousands of the most military class, peers, squires and their tenantry, who were enduring Anglicanism with its episcopate, its semi-Catholic prayer-book, and its claim to belong to the Universal Apostolic Church, because they could persuade themselves that its variations from the old religion were unimportant and temporary. And this again would increase the probability of foreign invasion. For, though to Philip all forms of heresy were equally damnable and equally marked out for extermination sooner or later, yet he was in much less hurry to begin with the politically harmless Lutherans or Anglicans than with the dangerous levellers who derived their inspiration from Geneva. Now for Elizabeth to gain time was everything. She had gained ten precious years already by her moderation. She was to gain twenty more before the slow-moving Spaniard decided to launch the great Armada.

But though Elizabeth shunned war with Spain she nevertheless recognised that Philip was the enemy, and that all ways of damaging him short of war were for her advantage. English and Huguenot corsairs swarmed in the Channel. Spanish ships were seized. The crews were hanged or made to walk the plank; the prizes were carried into English ports, and there sold without disguise or rebuke. These outrages were represented as reprisals for cruelties inflicted on English sailors who occasionally fell into the hands of the Inquisition. Practically a ship with a valuable cargo was treated as fair game whatever its nationality. But while in the case of other countries it was only individual traders who suffered, to Spain it meant obstruction of her high road to her Belgic dominions, then simmering with disaffection.

The English nobles of the old blood disliked these proceedings. Even Cecil did not conceal from himself that they fostered a spirit of lawlessness. What the corsairs were doing he would have preferred to see done by the royal navy. To that Elizabeth would not consent. The activity of the corsairs gave her all the advantage she could hope to have from war, without any of its disadvantages. Instead of laying out her treasure on a navy, she was deriving an income from the piratical ventures of Hawkins and Drake; while the ships and sailors of this volunteer navy would be available for the defence of the country whenever the need should arise. Whatever may be thought of the morality of her plan, there can be no question as to its efficiency and economy.

Since even these outrages, exasperating as they were, had not goaded Philip to the point of declaring war, a still more daring provocation now followed. Some ships, conveying a large sum of money borrowed by Philip in Genoa for the payment of Alva's army, having put into English ports to avoid the corsairs, Elizabeth, with the hearty approval of Cecil, took possession of the money, and said she would herself

borrow it from the Genoese (December 1568). The
Minister hoped this would bring on a war. The Queen
audaciously but more correctly anticipated that Philip's
resentment would still stop short of that extremity.
He remonstrated : he threatened : he seized all English ships and sailors in his ports. Elizabeth, undismayed, swept all the Spaniards and Flemings whom
she could find in London into her prisons, and seized
their goods, to a value far greater than that of the
English property in Philip's grasp.

In striking contrast with this unflinching attitude
towards Spain was the behaviour of Elizabeth when
threatened with war by France, unless she undertook
to close her harbours to the Huguenots, and to forbid
her own corsairs to prey on French commerce. The
summons was promptly obeyed. Full satisfaction was
made (April 1569). Yet France was at the moment
a far less formidable antagonist than Spain. The
French government did not possess the means of invading England. On this side of the Channel the old
anti-French feeling was so persistent that all parties
were ready and willing for the fray. The defeat of
the Huguenots at Jarnac (April 1569) may have had
something to do with Elizabeth's compliance. But
what influenced her still more was her perception that
war with France would compel her to place herself
under the protection of Spain ; whereas she desired to
keep Spain at arm's-length, and to maintain a good
understanding with France, as did Eliot, Pym, and
Cromwell afterwards, regardless of the rooted prejudices of their countrymen. Elizabeth probably stood
alone in her judgment on this occasion.

F

The quarrel with Philip had more serious results at home than abroad. It was indirectly the cause of the only English rebellion that disturbed the long reign of Elizabeth.

Most of the nobility and gentry, even when professedly Protestants, regretted the alienation of England from the Universal Church. If they had all pulled together they must have had their way, for they were the military and political class. But their discontent varied widely in its intensity. There were nobles like Sussex who were resolved to serve their Queen loyally and zealously, but who, all the same, wished her to cultivate a good understanding with Philip, to marry the Archduke, to abstain from assisting the Huguenots, to give no countenance to the rovers, to recognise Mary as her heir-presumptive and marry her to Norfolk. There were others like Norfolk, Montagu, Arundel, and Southampton, who had treasonable relations with the Spanish ambassador, and aimed at overthrowing Cecil, marrying Mary to Norfolk, and compelling the Queen to restore the Catholic worship, or at least to make such changes in the Anglican model as would facilitate a reunion with Rome when Mary should succeed. A third party, headed by the Catholic lords of the north, was plotting to depose Elizabeth in favour of Mary, and to marry the latter to Don John of Austria.

With these powerful nobles in opposition, who, before the Reformation, could have hurled any sovereign from his throne, where was Elizabeth to look for support? The town populations were Protestant —too Protestant indeed for her taste. But the town populations were a minority, and less military than the landowners and their tenants. She had her Cecils, Bacons, Walsinghams, Hunsdons, Knollyses, Sadlers, Killegrews, Drurys, capable and devoted servants, but new men without territorial wealth or influence, and with no force except what they possessed as wielding the power of the Crown. It would be difficult to name more than half-a-dozen peers who zealously promoted her policy. Most of them looked on it coldly, and would support her only as long as she seemed to be strongest.

Mary's rejection of Elizabeth's terms coincided with the quarrel with Philip (December 1568). The disaffected nobles thought that the time was now come for striking a blow. Conscious that the feudal devotion of the gentry and yeomanry to their local chiefs had in Tudor times been largely superseded by awe of the central government, they were importuning Philip to give them the signal for rebellion by sending a division of Alva's army from the Netherlands. Philip, cautious as usual, and afraid of driving England into alliance with France, declined to send a soldier until either the Norfolk party had overthrown Cecil, or the northern lords had carried off Mary. Between these two sets of conspirators there was much jealousy and distrust. The Spanish ambassador thought the southern scheme the most feasible. Not without difficulty he persuaded the northern lords to wait till it should be seen whether the Queen could be induced or compelled to sanction the marriage of Mary with Norfolk. If she refused, they were to make a dash on Wingfield, a seat of Lord Shrewsbury's in Derbyshire where Mary was staying, while Norfolk was to raise the eastern counties.

All through the summer of 1569 these plots were brewing. Three times Norfolk and his father-in-law Arundel went to the Council with the intention of arresting Cecil. Three times their hearts failed them. The northern lords, who were not members of the Council, came up to London to see Norfolk bell the cat, but went back, more suspicious than ever, to make their own preparations. Cecil himself seems to have been hedging. In his private advice to the Queen he was opposing the Norfolk marriage, pointing out that free or in prison, married or single, in England or in Scotland, Mary must always be dangerous, and breathing for the first time the suggestion that she might lawfully be put to death in England for complicity in English plots. In the Council he concurred in a vote that she should be married to an Englishman —in other words, to Norfolk.

If Elizabeth could have felt any confidence in Norfolk's loyalty, it seems probable that much as she disliked the marriage she would have yielded to the almost unanimous pronouncement of the nobility in its favour. But a sure instinct warned her of her danger. "If she consented she would be in the Tower before four months were over." After much deliberation she commanded the Duke on his allegiance to renounce his project. He gave his promise, but soon retired to his own county, and sent word to the northern earls that "he would stand and abide the venture." But while he was shivering and hesitating, Elizabeth, for once, was all promptitude and decision.

Mary was hurried to Tutbury Castle. Arundel and Pembroke were summoned to Windsor, and kept under surveillance. Norfolk himself came in quietly, and was lodged in the Tower. Thus the southern conspiracy collapsed (September-October 1569).

The Catholic lords and gentlemen of the north who had been awaiting Norfolk's signal, were staggered by his tame surrender. Sussex, who was in command at York, and who, being of the old blood himself, did not care to see old houses crushed, advised Elizabeth to wink at their half-begun treason, and be thankful it had not come to fighting. She winked at the attempted flight to Alva of Southampton and Montagu, and even affected to trust the latter with the command of the militia called out in Sussex. She could afford to ignore the disaffection of a southern noble. A Sussex squire or yeoman, even if he was not a Protestant, would think twice before he cast in his lot with rebellion. The northern counties were mainly Catholic. They were much behind the south in civilisation. The Tudor sovereigns were never seen there. Great families were still looked up to. Elizabeth knew that though rebellion might be adjourned, might possibly never come off, it was a constant menace, which crippled her policy. She determined therefore to have done with it, once for all, and summoned Northumberland and Westmoreland to London.

Thus driven into a corner, the two earls burst into rebellion. They entered Durham in arms, overthrew the communion table in the cathedral, set up the old altar, and had mass said (Nov. 14, 1569). Next day they marched south, with the object of rescuing Mary from Tutbury. But when they were within fifty miles of that place, Shrewsbury and Huntingdon, in obedience to hurried orders from London, conveyed her to Coventry. Having thus missed their spring, the rebel earls halted irresolutely for three days, and then turned back. Their followers dropped away from them. Clinton and Warwick were on their track, with the musters of the Midlands; and before the end of December they were fain to fly across the Border. Northumberland was arrested by Moray. Two years later he was given up to Elizabeth, and executed. Westmoreland, after being protected for a time by Ker of Ferniehirst, escaped to the Netherlands, where he died. [England was not again disturbed by rebellion till the great civil war.]

[The failure of the northern earls to kindle a general rebellion was due to the cautious and temporising policy for which Elizabeth has been so severely blamed by heated partisans. The powerful party which preferred a Spanish alliance, disliked religious innovation, and looked forward to the succession of Mary, had not been driven to despair of accomplishing those ends in a lawful way. Their avowed policy had not been proscribed—had not even been repudiated. Some of their chief leaders were on the Council—as we should say, were members of the Government; others were employed and trusted and visited by the Queen. They objected to being hurried into civil war by the northern lords, who were not of the Council, who kept away from London, and were rebels by inheritance and tradition. They would have nothing to do with the ill-advised movement; and, as in those days neutrality in the presence of open insurrection was no more permissible to a nobleman than it would be now to an officer in the army, they had no choice but to range themselves on the side of the Government. If Elizabeth had openly branded the Queen of Scots as a murderess, if she had pointed to Huntingdon or the son of Catherine Grey as her successor, if she had put herself at the head of a Protestant league, she might possibly have come victorious out of a civil war. But a civil war it would have been, and of the worst kind : one party calling in the Spaniard, and the other, in all probability, driven to call in the Frenchman.

The assassination of Moray a few weeks later (Jan. 23, 1570) was a severe blow to Elizabeth, and an irreparable disaster to his own country. An attempt has been made to create an impression that the English Queen was somehow responsible for his death, because she did not march an army into Scotland to support him. He no more wished to receive an English army into Scotland than Elizabeth wished to send one. Therein they were both of them wiser than the critics of their own day, or this. What he did ask for was money, and the recognition of James. The request for money Elizabeth was willing to consider, though, as a rule, she did not believe in paying for any work she could get done gratis. The recognition of James seems a very simple thing to the critics. But it was as difficult for Elizabeth as the recognition of the Prince of Bulgaria is now to Austria, and for similar reasons. She was under no obligation whatever to Moray. His own interest compelled him to play her game. But she well knew his value. On hearing of his death she shut herself up in her chamber, exclaiming, with tears, that she had lost the best friend she had in the world.

As long as Moray lived, and was able to keep the Marian lords in some sort of check, Elizabeth judged, and rightly, that she had more to lose than to gain by any open interference in Scotland. It was no business of hers to put down anarchy there. Scotch anarchy did not imperil England. What would imperil England would be the appearance of French troops in Scotland; and she judged that nothing would be so likely to bring them there as any pretension to establish an English protectorate. Her Protestant councillors fretted at her *laisser faire* policy. But then they, for personal or at least for sectarian reasons, were eager for that general European conflagration which she, with superior discernment and larger patriotism, was trying to avert.

The death of Moray so weakened the King's party that it became necessary to give them a little help. Elizabeth gave it in such a way as she thought would be least likely to excite the jealousy of France. She told the new Regent Lennox that, though she could not send an army to support him, she would send one to chastise the Hamiltons and the Borderers, who were harbouring her rebel the Earl of Westmoreland, and, along with him, making raids into England. This was done sharply and thoroughly. The robber holds on the Border, and Hamilton Castle itself, were one after another taken and blown up by the English Wardens of the Marches (April and May 1570).

What Elizabeth desired more than anything else

was to settle Scotch affairs, in conjunction with France, on the terms that neither power should interfere in Scotland. To Cecil this was unsatisfactory, because the restoration of Mary, on any terms whatever, would, if she survived Elizabeth, ensure her succession to the English throne, and the ruin of Cecil himself. He did not want to conciliate Catholics at home or abroad. He wanted to commit his mistress to an internecine war with them. In an angry dispute with Arundel at the Council board about this time, he blurted out his doctrine, that the Queen had no friends but the Protestants, and that if she restored Mary she would lose them all. No language could have been more displeasing to Elizabeth, especially in the presence of crypto-Catholic lords, and she snubbed him unmercifully. "Mr Secretary, I mean to have done with this business; I shall listen to the proposals of the French King. I am not going to be tied any longer to you and your brethren in Christ."

The peace of St. Germain between the French court and the Huguenots (August 8, 1570), and the disgrace of the Guises, were followed by negotiations for a tripartite treaty between England, France, and Scotland on the basis of the restoration of Mary. Elizabeth, of course, insisted on the guarantees she had often sketched out. She was willing—nay, anxious—to leave Scotland alone, if the French would do the same. The French, on the other hand, felt that the equality of such an arrangement was more seeming than real, because there were always English troops lying at Berwick, within sixty miles of Edinburgh. They haggled over the guarantees, and in the meantime, notwithstanding the real desire of Catherine and Charles IX. to conclude an alliance with Elizabeth against Philip, they continued to send money and encouragement to the Marian lords in Scotland. For if, for any reason, the English alliance should not come off, they meant to take up Mary's cause in earnest, and detach her from her Guise relations by marrying her to the Duke of Anjou, afterwards Henry III.

All this was known to Elizabeth, and in her extreme anxiety for the tripartite treaty, she thought the moment was come to dangle the bait which she always reserved for occasions of special importance. She informed the French ambassador that she was ready to marry Anjou herself. It is not to be supposed that she had the least intention of doing so. She had settled with herself from the first how she would get out of her proposal when it had served its turn.

A minor motive for this move was the hope that it would reconcile her Protestant councillors to the restoration of Mary. She did not succeed with all of them. Some continued to mutter that Anjou was a Papist, that tripartite treaties were a delusion, and that the only safe course was to grasp the Scotch nettle and uphold James with the whole force of England. But upon Cecil the effect was almost comical. He jumped at the plan. Anything that was likely to make Elizabeth a mother would be salvation to him. Whether the Queen at the mature age of thirty-seven was likely to be happy with a husband of twenty was a question that did not give him a moment's concern. She was not too old to have two or three children, and, that result once achieved, Mary might go to Scotland or anywhere else for what he cared, and do her worst. The sanguine man already saw visions of a converted Valois heading an Anglo-French crusade against Philip, and establishing the reformed faith throughout Europe. Walsingham his right-hand man, then ambassador at Paris, was equally bitten. This was in the year before the massacre of St. Bartholomew.

The overture of Elizabeth was very welcome to the French court. Negotiations for the match were soon opened, and continued during the first six months of 1571. At the same time, both the Scotch factions were summoned to accept the tripartite arrangement. Mary was at first eager for it, and instructed her agent, the Bishop of Ross, to swallow every condition that might be imposed. She looked on it as the only means of obtaining her release. But there is ample proof that she intended to throw its stipulations to the winds and fight for her own cause when once she should get back to Scotland. In playing this perfidious game, she had confidently counted on the help of France. The Regent's party, however, declined the treaty. They dreaded Mary's return, and they had no wish to shake hands with the Marian lords or admit them to a share in the Government. The tripartite scheme thus fell through. Mary herself ceased to care for it as soon as she heard of the projected match between Elizabeth and Anjou. She saw that if France was going to co-operate heartily with England, her sovereignty in Scotland would be merely nominal. She might almost as well remain with Lord Shrewsbury.

To remain quietly in England and be content with her position as heir-presumptive to the English crown was indeed the best and safest course open to her. She had only to acquiesce in it and give up plotting, and she might have lived here in considerable magnificence, and with as much freedom as she could desire. If she wished for a husband, she might have married any Englishman of whose loyalty Elizabeth could feel assured. It was of the greatest importance to both countries that she should bear more children. For it must be remembered that if James had died in his childhood, his next heir was a Hamilton, who had no title to the English throne.

If the proposed Anjou match had not produced the full results which Elizabeth hoped, it had at least defeated the plans and disorganised the party of her rival. It had served its turn; and all that now remained was to get out of it as decently as possible. The old pretext for breaking off the Austrian match was reproduced. Anjou could not be allowed to have a private mass; and when, in its eagerness, the French court seemed disposed to give way on this point, Elizabeth began to talk about a restitution of Calais. Ruefully did poor Cecil watch the vanishing of his dream. It was to no purpose that he tried to frighten Elizabeth by representing that a jilted prince would be converted into an angry enemy. She knew better. Anjou comprehended that she did not mean to have him, and, to avoid the indignity of a refusal, himself broke off negotiations. But, as Elizabeth had calculated, the new alliance did not suffer. The French King went out of his way to say that "for her upright dealing he would honour the Queen of England during his life," and Catherine, most unsentimental of women, had another suitor to offer—her youngest son Alençon, then just turned seventeen!

While the negotiations for the Anjou match were going on, what is known as the Ridolfi Plot was hatching against Elizabeth. Ridolfi, an Italian banker in London, and secretly an agent of the Pope, was in close relations with Norfolk and the other peers who for two years had been dabbling in treason. They were still pressing Philip to invade England; but he and Alva were less than ever disposed to undertake the venture since the pitiful collapse of the northern insurrection. In order to impress Philip with the importance of the conspiracy, Ridolfi went to Madrid, and showed Philip a letter purporting to be written by Norfolk, to which was attached a list of noblemen stated to be favourable to the cause. It contained the names of forty out of the sixty-seven peers then existing, while, of the rest, some were marked as neutral, and fifteen at most as true to Elizabeth. The classification was on the face of it absurdly untrustworthy. But correct or incorrect, it did not weigh with Philip. He wanted deeds, not lists of names, and Ridolfi was informed that, unless Elizabeth were first assassinated or imprisoned, not a Spanish soldier could be sent to England.

Whatever secret disaffection might prevail among the peers, the temper displayed by the new House of Commons, elected in the spring of 1571, was not of a kind to encourage Elizabeth's enemies at home or abroad. So far as can be judged from its proceedings and debates, it was not only entirely Protestant, but largely Puritan.[1] A bill was passed by which any person refusing, on demand, to acknowledge Elizabeth's right to the crown was made incapable of succeeding her; a provision which, though it did not name Mary, could apply to no one else. It was made high treason to deny that the inheritance of the crown could be determined by the Queen and Parliament. To affirm in writing that any particular person was entitled to succeed the Queen, except the Queen's issue, or some one established by Parliament, was made punishable with imprisonment for life, and forfeiture of all property for the second offence.

The plot which Ridolfi was so busily pushing in 1571 was, in fact, a continuation of the twin aristocratic conspiracies, one of which had exploded in the northern insurrection. By forcing that insurrection to break out before the southern conspirators had made up their minds what to do, the Government had effectually destroyed what chances of success the disaffected nobles had ever had. Alva was right in his judgment that, if the Percys, Nevilles, and Dacres could do so little, the Howard group, whose estates, vast as they were, lay, for the most part, in more orderly and civilised parts of the country, could do still less. There was, indeed, some talk among them of seizing the Queen at the opening of the Parliament of 1571, just as there had been a talk of arresting Cecil two years before. But the truth was that insurrection was a played-out game in England;

[1] The oath of supremacy imposed on members of the House of Commons in 1562 practically excluded conscientious Catholics.

and if Norfolk had been a ten-times abler and bolder man than he was, it would have made no difference.

The true history of the time is not to be read in the croakings and wailings privately exchanged between Cecil, Walsingham, and the rest of the Protestant junto, angry and alarmed because Elizabeth would not let them play her cards for her. It is a strange perversity which persists in adopting their view that she was on the brink of ruin, when the patent fact is that Protestantism was making rapid strides, that the Queen's personal popularity was increasing every day, and that Spain, France, and Scotland, the only countries with which she was concerned, were all humble suitors for her alliance on almost any terms that it might please her to exact. The correspondence of Philip with Alva is there to prove, that while writhing under the repeated aggressions of England, he was obliged to put up with them because a war would imperil his hold on the Netherlands. To all the invitations of the Norfolks and Northumberlands, the able and well-informed Alva turned a deaf ear, because he believed Elizabeth too strong to be overthrown. A French alliance she could always have as long as the Guises were excluded from power. If they regained their influence the Huguenots would keep them fully occupied. Scotland, unless foreign troops made their appearance there, could be no source of danger to England.

Elizabeth's policy was thus, in its broad lines, as simple as it was successful. At home it was her wisdom to wink as long as possible at the disaffection of the few, to win the affection of the many by economical government, to reserve the persecuting laws for special cases, while preventing any general and sweeping application of them, and, lastly, to drive no party to desperation by a too pronounced encouragement of its opponents. Spain, as being the centre of reaction and the hope of her disloyal nobles, she meant to harass and weaken as far as she could do so without bringing on an open war. With Charles IX. and his mother she desired a defensive alliance, and an understanding that neither country should send troops into Scotland or permit Spain to do so. In its general conception, I repeat, this policy was simple and coherent. How it succeeded we know. There was nothing sentimental about it, though, where individuals were concerned, Elizabeth's judgment was sometimes warped by sentiment. Upon the whole, she kept herself at the English point of view. Whereas Cecil was compelled by personal considerations to place himself too much at the point of view of his "brethren in Christ," both at home and abroad.

However, a plot there was, and it was necessary that it should be unravelled and punished. Almost from its inception, Cecil (created Lord Burghley February 1571), had been more or less on the scent of it. Hints had come from abroad: spies had been employed: suspected persons had been closely watched: inferior agents had been imprisoned, questioned, racked: and enough had been discovered to make it certain that Englishmen of the highest rank were plotting treason. Who they were might be suspected, but was not ascertained until a lucky arrest put the Minister in possession of evidence incriminating Norfolk, Arundel, Southampton, Lumley, Cobham, the Spanish ambassador, the Bishop of Ross, and Mary herself (September 1571). Norfolk was sent to the Tower, and the other peers placed under arrest. The ambassador was dismissed. The Bishop made ample confessions. Mary, who had hitherto lived as the guest of Lord Shrewsbury, enjoying field-sports, receiving her friends and corresponding with whom she would, was confined to a single room, and carefully cut off, for a time, from all communication with the outer world. Both in England and abroad it was universally expected that she would be brought to trial and executed. James was at length officially styled "King" and his mother "late Queen." Her partisans in Edinburgh Castle were informed that she would never be restored, and that, if they did not surrender the Castle to the Regent Mar, an English force would be sent to take it. The casket letters had hitherto been withheld from publication under pressure from Elizabeth; they were now at last given to the world in the famous "Detection" of Buchanan.

Under any other Tudor, or under the Stuarts, all the peers arrested would undoubtedly have lost their heads. Norfolk alone was brought to trial (January 1572). There was much in the proceedings which, according to modern notions, was unfair to the accused. But the peers who tried him felt sure that he was guilty, and they were right. Subsequent investigations have established beyond a doubt that he had conspired to bring a foreign army into the country—the worst form that treason can take. He had done this with contemptible hypocrisy, for a purely selfish object, and after the most lenient and generous construction had been placed on his first steps in crime. And yet historians have been found to make light of the offence, and to pity the malefactor as the victim of a romantic attachment to a woman whom he had never seen, and whom he believed to be an adulteress and a murderess.

During the spring of 1572 Elizabeth hesitated to let justice take its course. She had reigned fourteen years without taking the life of a single noble. The scaffold on Tower Hill from such long disuse was falling to pieces, and Norfolk's sentence had made it necessary to erect a new one. Elizabeth was loath to break the spell.

Not knowing with any certainty how many of her nobles might have given more or less approval to the Ridolfi plot, but confident that she could cow them by letting the voice of the untitled aristocracy and middle class be heard, she called a new Parliament (May 1572). The response went beyond her expectation. Of Mary's well-wishers, once so numerous, all except a few fanatics had now given her up. Two alternative courses of action with respect to her were submitted for consideration, with the intimation that the Queen would accept whichever of them Parliament should approve. The first was attainder. The second was that she should be disabled from succession to the crown; that if she attempted treason again she should "suffer pains of death without further trouble of Parliament;" and that it should be treason if she assented to any enterprise to deliver her out of prison. Both houses at once voted to proceed with the attainder. Elizabeth, we may be sure, was not sorry for this unmistakable exhibition of feeling. It would open the eyes of her enemies both at home and abroad. But she had no intention of proceeding to such extremities this time. Mary should have fair warning. Accordingly Parliament was desired to "defer" the bill of attainder, and to proceed with the second measure. But the Commons were in grim earnest. They immediately resolved that the second bill would be useless and even mischievous, as it would imply that at present Mary had a right of succession, whereas she was already disabled by law; and that they therefore preferred to proceed with the attainder. With this resolution the Lords concurred.

Here they were on dangerous ground. To rake up the law empowering Henry VIII. to determine the succession was to disable all the Stuarts, James included, and so to throw away the opportunity of uniting the crowns. Elizabeth had always, for excellent reasons, refused to allow this question to be raised. Accordingly she again directed the House to defer the attainder; she would not have the Scottish Queen " either enabled or disabled to or from any manner of *title* to the crown," nor "any other *title* to the same whatsoever touched at all;" to make sure of which she would have the second bill drawn by her own law officers. To the repeated demands of the Commons for the execution of Norfolk, she at length gave way, and a few days later he was beheaded (June 2, 1572). The second bill, as drawn by the law officers, passed both Houses. Its exact terms are not known, for it never received the royal assent.

Burghley who was of opinion (as some one afterwards said about Strafford) that "stone dead hath no fellow," bemoaned himself privately to Walsingham on the disappointment of their hopes; and modern historians, with whom his authority is final, are loud in their condemnation of Elizabeth's vacillation and blindness. Vacillation there was really none. She had determined from the first not to allow Mary to be punished. She had gained all she wanted when the temper of Parliament had been ascertained and displayed to the world. There have always been plenty of people to accuse her of treachery and cruelty because she put Mary to death fifteen years later, for complicity in an assassination plot. How would her name have gone down to posterity if the Scottish Queen had been executed in 1572 merely for inviting a foreign army to rescue her from captivity ?

CHAPTER VI

FOREIGN AFFAIRS : 1572-1583

THE year 1572 witnessed two events of capital importance in European history: the rising in the Netherlands, which resulted in the establishment of the Dutch Republic (April); and the massacre of St. Bartholomew, which marked the decisive rejection of Protestantism by France (August).

In the beginning of that year—a few weeks before the proceedings in Parliament just narrated—Elizabeth had at last concluded the defensive alliance with France for which she had been so long negotiating (April 19). It cannot be too often repeated that this was the corner-stone of her foreign policy. For the sake of its superior importance she had abstained from the interference in Scotland which her Ministers were always urging. The more she interfered there the more she would have to interfere, till it would end in her having a rebellious province on her hands in addition to the hostility of both France and Spain; whereas an alliance with France would give her security on all sides, Scotland included. In the treaty it was agreed that if either country were invaded "under any pretence or cause, none excepted," the other should send 6000 troops to its assistance. This was accompanied with an explanation, in the King's handwriting, that "any cause" included religion. The article relating to Scotland is not less significant. The two sovereigns "shall make no innovations in Scotland, but defend it against foreigners, not suffering strangers to enter, or foment the factions in Scotland; but it shall be lawful for the Queen of England to chastise by arms the Scots who shall countenance the English rebels now in Scotland." Mary was not mentioned. France therefore tacitly renounced her cause. Immediately after the conclusion of the treaty Charles IX. formally proposed a marriage between Elizabeth and his youngest brother, Alençon. This proposal she managed to encourage and elude for eleven years.

It was just at this moment that the seizure of Brill by some Dutch rovers, who had taken refuge on the sea from the cruelty of Alva, caused most of the towns of Holland and Zealand to blaze into rebellion (April 1). Thus began the great war of liberation, which was to last thirty-seven years. The Protestant party in England hailed the revolt with enthusiasm. Large subscriptions were made to assist it, and volunteers poured across to take part in the struggle. Charles IX. and his mother, full of schemes of conquest in the Netherlands, urged Elizabeth to join them in a war against Philip. But, with a sagacity and self-restraint which do her infinite honour, she refused to be drawn beyond the lines laid down in the recent defensive alliance. Security, economy, fructification of the tax-payers' money in the tax-payers' pocket—such were the guiding principles of her policy. She was not to be dragged into dangerous enterprises either ambitious or Quixotic. Schemes for the partition of the Netherlands were laid before her. Zealand, it was said, would indemnify her for Calais. What Englishman with any common sense does not now see that she was right to reject the bribe?

To Elizabeth no rebellion against a legitimate sovereign could be welcome in itself. Since Philip was so possessed by religious bigotry as to be dangerous to all Protestant States, she was not sorry that he should wear out his crusading ardour in the Netherlands; and she was ready to give just as much assistance to the Dutch, in an underhand way, as would keep him fully occupied without bringing a declaration of war upon herself. But she would have vastly preferred that he should repress Catholic and Protestant fanatics alike, and get along quietly with the mass of his subjects as his father had done before him. Charles IX. was eager to strike in if she would join him. Those who blame her so severely for her refusal seem to forget that a French conquest of the Netherlands would have been far more dangerous to this country than their possession by Spain. To keep them out of French hands has indeed been the traditional policy of England during the whole of modern history.

But, it is said, such a war would have clinched the alliance recently patched up between the French court and the Huguenots; there would have been no Bartholomew Massacre; "on Elizabeth depended at that moment whether the French Government would take its place once for all on the side of the Reformation."

Whether it would have been for the advantage of European progress in the long-run that France should settle down into Calvinism, I will forbear to inquire. Fortunately for the immediate interests of England, Elizabeth understood the situation in France better than some of her critics do, even with the results before their eyes. The Huguenots were but a small fraction of the nation. Whatever importance they possessed they derived from their rank, their turbulence, and the ambition of their leaders. In a few towns of the south and south-west they formed a majority of the population. But everywhere else they were mostly noblemen, full of the arrogance and reckless valour of their class, anything but puritans in their morals, and ready to destroy the unity of the kingdom for political no less than for religious objects. They had been losing ground for several years. The mass of the people abhorred their doctrines, and protested against any concession to their pretensions. Charles and his mother were absolutely careless about religion. Their feud with the Guises and their designs on the Netherlands had led them to invite the Huguenot chiefs to court, and so to give them a momentary influence in shaping the policy of France. It was with nothing more solid to lean on than this ricketty and short-lived combination that Burghley and Walsingham were eager to launch England into a war with the most powerful monarchy in Europe.

The massacre of St. Bartholomew (August 24) was a rude awakening from these dreams. That thunderclap did not show that, in signing the treaty with England and in proposing an attack on Philip, the French Government had been playing a treacherous game all along, in order to lure the Huguenots to the shambles. But it did show that when the Catholic sentiment in France was thoroughly roused, the dynasty itself must bend before it or be swept away. England might help the Huguenots to keep up a desultory and harassing civil war; she could no more enable them to control the policy of the French nation and wield its force, than she could at the present day restore the Bourbons or Bonapartes.

The first idea of Elizabeth and her ministers, on receiving the news of the massacre, naturally was that the French Government had been playing them false from the first, that the Catholic League for the extirpation of heresy in Europe, which had been so much talked of since the Bayonne interview in 1565, was after all a reality, and that England might expect an attack from the combined forces of Spain and France. Thanks to the prudent policy of Elizabeth, England was in a far better position to meet all dangers than she had been in 1565. The fleet was brought round to the Downs. The coast was guarded by militia. An expedition was organised to co-operate with the Dutch insurgents. Money was sent to the Prince of Orange. Huguenot refugees were allowed to fit out a flotilla to assist their co-religionists in Rochelle. The Scotch Regent Mar was informed, with great secrecy, that if he would demand the extradition of Mary, and undertake to punish her capitally for her husband's murder, she should be given up to him.

A few weeks sufficed to show that there was no reason for panic. Confidence, indeed, between the French and English Governments had been severely shaken. Each stood suspiciously on its guard. But the alliance was too well grounded in the interests of both parties to be lightly cast aside. The French ambassador was instructed to excuse and deplore the massacre as best he could, and to press on the Alençon marriage. Elizabeth, dressed in deep mourning, gave him a stiff reception, but let him see her desire to maintain the alliance. The massacre did not restore the ascendancy of the Guises. To the Huguenots, as religious reformers, it gave a blow from which they did not recover. But as a political faction they were not crushed. Nay, their very weakness became their salvation, since it compelled them to fall into the second rank behind the *Politiques*, the true party of progress, who were before long to find a victorious leader in Henry of Navarre.

Philip, for his part, was equally far from any thought of a crusade against England. Sir Humphrey Gilbert, commanding several companies of English volunteers, with the hardly concealed sanction of his government, was fighting against the Spaniards in Walcheren and hanging all his prisoners. Sir John Hawkins, with twenty ships, had sailed to intercept the Mexican treasure fleet. Yet Alva, though gnashing his teeth, was obliged to advise his master to swallow it all, and to be thankful if he could get Elizabeth to reopen commercial intercourse, which had been prohibited on both sides since the quarrel about the Genoese treasure. A treaty for this purpose was in fact concluded early in 1573. Thus the chief result of the Bartholomew Massacre, as far as Elizabeth was concerned, was to show how strong her position was, and that she had no need either to truckle to Catholics or let her hand be forced by Protestants. A balance of power on the Continent was what suited her, as it has generally suited this country. Let her critics say what they will, it was no business of hers to organise a Protestant league, and so drive the Catholic sovereigns to sink their mutual jealousies and combine against the common enemy.

The Scotch Regent was quite ready to undertake the punishment of Mary, but only on condition that Elizabeth would send the Earl of Bedford or the Earl of Huntingdon with an army to be present at the execution and to take Edinburgh Castle. It need hardly be said that there was also a demand for money. Mar died during the negotiations, but they were continued by his successor Morton. Elizabeth was determined to give no open consent to Mary's execution. She meant, no doubt, as soon as it should be over, to protest, as she did fifteen years afterwards, that there had been an unfortunate mistake, and to lay the blame of it on the Scotch Government and her own agents. This part of the negotiation therefore came to nothing. But money was sent to Morton, which enabled him to establish a blockade of Edinburgh Castle, and by the mediation of Elizabeth's ambassador, the Hamiltons, Gordons, and all the other Marians except those in the Castle, accepted the very favourable terms offered them, and recognised James.

All that remained was to reduce the Castle. Its

defenders numbered less than two hundred men. The city and the surrounding country were—as far as preaching and praying went—vehemently anti-Marian. The Regent had now no other military task on his hands. Elizabeth might well complain when she was told that unless she sent an army and paid the Scotch Protestants to co-operate with it, the Castle could not be taken. For some time she resisted this thoroughly Scotch demand. But at last she yielded to Morton's importunity. Sir William Drury marched in from Berwick, did the job, and marched back again (May 1573). Among the captives were the brilliant Maitland of Lethington, once the most active of Anglophiles, and Kirkaldy of Grange, who had begun the Scottish Reformation by the murder of Cardinal Beaton, and had taken Mary prisoner at Carberry Hill. A politician who did not turn his coat at least once in his life was a rare bird in Scotland. Maitland died a few days after his capture, probably by his own hand. Kirkaldy was hanged by his old friend Morton.

By taking Edinburgh Castle Elizabeth did not earn any gratitude from the party who had called her in. What they wanted, and always would want, was money. Morton himself, treading in the steps of his old leader Moray, remained an unswerving Anglophile. But his coadjutors told the English ambassador plainly that, if they could not get money from England, they could and would earn it from France. Elizabeth's councillors were always teasing her to comply with these impudent demands. If there had been a grown-up King on the throne, a man with a will of his own, and whose right to govern could not be contested, it might have been worth while to secure his good-will by a pension; and this was what Elizabeth did when James became real ruler of the country. But she did not believe in paying a clique of greedy lords to call themselves the English party. An English party there was sure to be, if only because there was a French party. Their services would be neither greater nor smaller whether they were paid or unpaid. The French poured money into Scotland, and were worse served than Elizabeth, who kept her money in her treasury. It was no fault of Elizabeth if the conditions of political life in Scotland during the King's minority were such that a firmly established government was in the nature of things impossible.

As Mary was kept in strict seclusion during the panic that followed on the Bartholomew Massacre, she did not know how narrow was her escape from a shameful death on a Scottish scaffold. When the panic subsided she was allowed to resume her former manner of life as the honoured guest of Lord Shrewsbury, with full opportunities for communication with all her friends at home and abroad. Any alarm she had felt speedily disappeared. If Elizabeth had for a moment contemplated striking at her life or title by parliamentary procedure, that intention was evidently abandoned when the Parliament of 1572 was prorogued without any such measure becoming law. The public assumed, and rightly, that Elizabeth still regarded the Scottish Queen as her successor. Peter Wentworth in the next session (1576) asserted, and probably with truth, that many who had been loud in their demands for severity repented of their forwardness when they found that Mary might yet be their Queen, and tried to make their peace with her. Wentworth's outburst (for which he was sent to the Tower) was the only demonstration against Mary in that session. She told the Archbishop of Glasgow that her prospects had never been better, and when opportunities for secret escape were offered her she declined to use them, thinking that it was for her interest to remain in England.

The desire of the English Queen to reinstate her rival arose principally from an uneasy consciousness that, by detaining her in custody, she was fatally impairing that religious respect for sovereigns which was the main, if not the only, basis of their power. The scaffold of Fotheringay was, in truth, the prelude to the scaffold of Whitehall. But as year succeeded year, and Elizabeth became habituated to the situation which had at first given her such qualms, she could not shut her eyes to the fact that, troublesome and even dangerous as Mary's presence in England was, the trouble and the danger had been very much greater when she was seated on the Scottish throne. The seething caldron of Scotch politics had not, indeed, become a negligible quantity. It required watching. But experience had shown that, while the King was a child, the Scots were neither valuable as friends nor formidable as foes. This was a truth quite as well understood at Paris and Madrid as at London, though the French, no less keen in those days than they are now to maintain that shadowy thing called "legitimate French influence" in countries with which they had any historical connection, continued to intrigue and waste their money among the hungry Scotch nobles. It was a fixed principle with Elizabeth, as with all English statesmen, not to tolerate the presence of foreign troops in Scotland. But she believed—and her belief was justified by events—that a French expedition was not the easy matter it had been when Mary of Guise was Regent of Scotland and Mary Tudor Queen of England. And, more important still, in spite of much treachery and distrust, the French and English Governments were bound together by a treaty which was equally necessary to each of them. Scotland, therefore, was no longer such a cause of anxiety to Elizabeth as it had been during the first ten years of her reign. Her ministers had neither her coolness nor her insight. Yet modern historians, proud of having unearthed their croaking criticisms, ask us to judge Elizabeth's policy by prognostications which turned out to be false rather than by the known results which so brilliantly justified it.

How to deal with the Netherlands was a much more complicated and difficult problem. Here again Elizabeth's ministers were for carrying matters with a high hand. In their view, England was in constant danger of a Spanish invasion, which could only be averted by openly and vigorously supporting the revolted provinces. They would have had Elizabeth place herself at the head of a Protestant league, and dare the worst that Philip could do. She, on the other hand, believed that every year war could be delayed was so much gained for England. There were many ways in which she could aid the Netherlands without openly challenging Philip. A curious theory of international relations prevailed in those days—an English Prime Minister, by the way, found it convenient not long ago to revive it—according to which, [to carry on warlike operations against another country was a very different thing from going to war with that country. Of this theory Elizabeth largely availed herself. English generals were not only allowed, but encouraged, to raise regiments of volunteers to serve in the Low Countries. When there, they reported to the English Government, and received instructions from it with hardly a pretence of concealment. Money was openly furnished to the Prince of Orange. English fleets— also nominally of volunteers—were encouraged to prey on Spanish commerce, Elizabeth herself subscribing to their outfit and sharing in the booty.]

[We are not to suppose, because the revolt of the Netherlands crippled Philip for any attack on England, that Elizabeth welcomed it, or that she contemplated the prolongation of the struggle with cold-blooded satisfaction. Its immediate advantage to this country was obvious. But Elizabeth had a sincere abhorrence of war and disorder. She was equally provoked with Philip for persecuting the Dutch Protestants into rebellion, and with the Dutch for insisting on religious concessions which Philip could not be expected to grant, and which she herself was not granting to Catholics in England. At any time during the struggle, if Philip would have guaranteed liberty of conscience (as distinguished from liberty of public worship), the restoration of the old charters, and the removal of the Spanish troops, Elizabeth would not only have withheld all help from the Dutch, but would have put pressure on them to submit to Philip. The presence of Spanish veterans opposite the mouth of the Thames was a standing menace to England. "As they are there," argued Burghley, "we must help the Dutch to keep them employed." "If the Dutch were not such impracticable fanatics," rejoined Elizabeth, "the Spanish veterans need not be there at all."..

The "Pacification of Ghent" (November 1576), by which the Belgian Netherlands, for a short time, made common cause with Holland and Zealand, relieved Elizabeth, for a time, from the necessity of taking any decisive step. Philip was still recognised as sovereign, but he was required to be content with such powers as the old constitution gave him. It seemed likely that Catholic bigots would have to give up persecuting, and Protestant bigots to acquiesce in the official establishment of the old religion. This was precisely the settlement Elizabeth had always desired. It would get rid of the Spanish troops. It would keep out the French. It would relieve her from the necessity of interfering. If it put some restriction on the open profession of Calvinism she would not be sorry.

If this arrangement could have been carried out, would it in the long-run have been for the benefit of Europe? Those who hold that the conflict between Protestantism and Catholicism was simply a conflict between truth and falsehood will, of course, have no difficulty in giving their answer. Others may hold that freedom of conscience was all that was needed at the time, and they may picture the many advantages which Europe would have reaped during the last three centuries from the existence of a united Netherlands, independent, as it must soon have become, of Spain, and able to make its independence respected by its neighbours.

Short-lived as the coalition was destined to be, it secured for the Dutch a breathing-time when they were most sorely pressed, and enabled Elizabeth to avoid quarrelling with Spain. The first step of the newly allied States was to apply to her for assistance and a loan of money. The loan they obtained— £40,000—a very large sum in those days. But she earnestly advised them that if the new Governor, Don John of Austria, would accept the Pacification, they should use the money to pay the arrears of the Spanish troops; otherwise they would refuse to leave the country for Don John or any one else. This was done. Don John had treachery in his heart. But the departure of the Spaniards was a solid gain; and if the Protestants and Catholics of the Netherlands had been able to tolerate each other, they would have achieved the practical independence of their country, and achieved it by their own unaided efforts.

But Don John, the crusader, the victor of Lepanto, the half-brother of Philip, was a man of soaring ambition. His dream was to invade England, marry the Queen of Scots, and seat himself with her on the English throne. It was in vain that Philip, who never wavered in his desire to conciliate Elizabeth, and was jealous of his showy brother, had strictly enjoined him to leave England alone. He persisted in his design, and sent his confidant Escovedo to persuade Philip that to conquer the Netherlands it was necessary to begin by conquering England.

For a pair of determined enemies, Elizabeth and Philip were just now upon most amicable, not to say affectionate, terms. She knew well that he had incited assassins to take her life, and that nothing would at any time give him greater pleasure than to hear that one of them had succeeded. But she bore him no malice for that. She took it all in the way of business, and intended, for her part, to go on robbing and damaging him in every way she could short of going to war. Philip bore it all meekly. Alva himself insisted that he could not afford to quarrel with her. Diplomatic relations by means of resident ambassadors, which had been broken off by the expulsion of De Espes in 1571, were resumed; and English heretics in the prisons of the Inquisition were released in spite of the outcries of the Grand Inquisitor.

In the summer of 1577 it seemed as if Don John's restless ambition would interrupt this pacific policy which suited both monarchs. He had sent for the Spanish troops again. He was known to be projecting an invasion of England. He was said to have a promise of help from Guise. Elizabeth's ministers, as usual, believed that she was on the brink of ruin, and implored her to send armies both to the Netherlands and to France. But she refused to be hustled into any precipitate action, and reasons soon appeared for maintaining an expectant attitude. The treaty of Bergerac between Henry III. and Henry of Navarre (September 1577) showed once more that the French

King had no intention of letting the Huguenots be crushed. The invitation of the Archduke Matthias by the Belgian nobles showed that they were deeply jealous of English interference. Here, surely, was matter for reflection. The most Elizabeth could be got to do was to become security for a loan of £100,000 to the States, on condition that Matthias should leave the real direction of affairs to William of Orange, and to *promise* armed assistance (January 1578). At the same time she informed Philip that she was obliged to do this for her own safety; that she had no desire to contest his sovereignty of the Netherlands; on the contrary, she would help him to maintain it if he would govern reasonably; but he ought to remove Don John, who was her mortal enemy, and to appoint another Governor of his own family; in other words, Matthias. Her policy could not have been more candidly set forth, and Philip showed his disapproval of Don John's designs in a characteristic way—by causing Escovedo to be assassinated. Don John himself died in the autumn, of a fever brought on by disappointment, or, as some thought, of a complaint similar to Escovedo's (September 1578).

When Elizabeth feared that Don John's scheme was countenanced by his brother, she had risked an open rupture by promising to send an army to the Netherlands. The murder of Escovedo and the arrival of the Spanish ambassador Mendoza (March 1578) reassured her. Philip was evidently pacific to the point of tameness. Instead, therefore, of sending an English army, she preferred to pay John Casimir, the Count Palatine, to lead a German army to the assistance of the States. As far as military strength went, they were probably no losers by the change. But what they wanted was to see Elizabeth committed to open war with Philip, and that was just what she desired to avoid. Indirect and underhand blows she was prepared to deal him, for she knew by experience that he would put up with them. Thus in the preceding autumn she had despatched Drake on his famous expedition to the South Pacific.

Don John was succeeded by his nephew, Alexander of Parma. The fine prospects of the revolted provinces were now about to be dashed. In the arts which smooth over difficulties and conciliate opposition, Parma had few equals. He was a head and shoulders above all contemporary generals; and no soldiers of that time were comparable to his Spanish and Italian veterans. When he assumed the command, he was master of only a small corner of the Low Countries. What he effected is represented by their present division between Belgians and Dutch. The struggle in the Netherlands continued, therefore, to be the principal object of Elizabeth's attention.

Shortly before the death of Don John, the Duke of Alençon,[1] brother and heir-presumptive of Henry III. had been invited by the Belgian nobles to become their Protector, and Orange, in his anxiety for union, had accepted their nominee. Alençon was to furnish 12,000 French troops. It was hoped and believed that, though Henry had ostensibly disapproved of his brother's action, he would in the end give him open

[1] He had received the Duchy of Anjou in addition to that of Alençon, and some historians call him by the former title.

support, thus resuming the enterprise which had been interrupted six years before by the Bartholomew Massacre.

Now, how was Elizabeth to deal with this new combination? The Protectorship of Alençon might bring on annexation to France, the result which most of all she wished to avoid. For a moment she thought of offering her own protection (which Orange would have much preferred), and an army equal to that promised by Alençon. But upon further reflection, she determined to adhere to the policy of not throwing down the glove to Philip, and to try whether she could not put Alençon in harness, and make him do her work. One means of effecting this would be to allow him subsidies—the means employed on such a vast scale by Pitt in our wars with Napoleon. But Elizabeth intended to spend as little as possible in this way. She relied chiefly on a revival of the marriage comedy—now to be played positively for the last time; the lady being forty-five, and her wooer twenty-four.

A dignified policy it certainly was not. All that was ridiculous and repulsive in her coquetry with Henry had now to be repeated and outdone with his younger brother. To overcome the incredulity which her previous performances had produced, she was obliged to exaggerate her protestations, to admit a personal courtship, to simulate amorous emotion, and to go through a tender pantomime of kisses and caresses. But Elizabeth never let dignity stand in the way of business. What to most women would have been an insupportable humiliation did not cost her a pang. She even found amusement in it. From the nature of the case, she could not take one of her counsellors into her confidence. There was no chance of imposing upon foreigners unless she could persuade those about her that she was in earnest. They were amazed that she should run the risk of establishing the French in the Netherlands. She had no intention of doing so. When Philip should be brought so low as to be willing to concede a constitutional government, she could always throw her weight on his side and get rid of the French.

The match with Alençon had been proposed six years before. It had lately slumbered. But there was no difficulty in whistling him back, and making it appear that the renewed overture came from his side. After tedious negotiations, protracted over twelve months, he at length paid his first visit to Elizabeth (August 1579). He was an under-sized man with an over-sized head, villainously ugly, with a face deeply seamed by smallpox, a nose ending in a knob that made it look like two noses, and a croaking voice. Elizabeth's liking for big handsome men is well known. But as she had not the least intention of marrying Alençon, it cost her nothing to affirm that she was charmed with his appearance, and that he was just the sort of man she could fancy for a husband. The only agreeable thing about him was his conversation, in which he shone, so that people who did not thoroughly know him always at first gave him credit for more ability than he possessed. Elizabeth, who had a pet name for all favourites, dubbed him her "frog"; and "Grenouille" he was fain to subscribe himself in his love-letters. This first visit was a short one, and he went away hopeful of success.

The English people could only judge by appearances, and for the first time in her reign Elizabeth was unpopular. The Puritan Stubbs published his *Discovery of a Gaping Gulf wherein England is like to be swallowed by another French Marriage.* But the excitement was by no means confined to the Puritans. Hatred of Frenchmen long remained a ruling sentiment with most Englishmen. Elizabeth vented her rage on Stubbs, who had been so rude as to tell her that childbirth at her age would endanger her life. He was sentenced to have his hand cut off. "I remember," says Camden, "being then present, that Stubbs, after his right hand was cut off, put off his hat with his left, and said with a loud voice, 'God save the Queen.' The multitude standing about was deeply silent."

Not long after Alençon's visit, a treaty of marriage was signed (November 1579), with a proviso that two months should be allowed for the Queen's subjects to become reconciled to it. If, at the end of that time, Elizabeth did not ratify the treaty, it was to be null and void. The appointed time came and went without ratification. Burghley, as usual, predicted that the jilted suitor would become a deadly enemy, and drew an alarming picture of the dangers that threatened England, with the old exhortation to his mistress to form a Protestant league and subsidise the Scotch Anglophiles. But in 1572 she had slipped out of the Anjou marriage, and yet secured a French alliance. She confided in her ability to play the same game now. Though she had not ratified the marriage treaty, she continued to correspond with Alençon and keep up his hopes, urging him at the same time to lead an army to the help of the States. This, however, he was unwilling to do till he had secured the marriage. The French King was ready, and even eager, to back his brother. But he, too, insisted on the marriage, and that Elizabeth should openly join him in war against Spain.

In the summer of 1580, Philip conquered Portugal, thus not only rounding off his Peninsular realm, but acquiring the enormous transmarine dominions of the Portuguese crown. All Europe was profoundly impressed and alarmed by this apparent increase of his power. Elizabeth incessantly lectured Henry on the necessity of abating a preponderance so dangerous to all other States, and tried to convince him that it was specially incumbent on France to undertake the enterprise. But she preached in vain. Henry steadily refused to stir unless England would openly assist him with troops and money, of which the marriage was to be the pledge. He did not conceal his suspicion that, when Elizabeth had pushed him into war, she would "draw her neck out of the collar" and leave him to bear the whole danger.

This was, in fact, her intention. She believed that a war with France would soon compel Philip to make proper concessions to the States; whereupon she would interpose and dictate a peace. "Marry my brother," Henry kept saying, "and then I shall have security that you will bear your fair share of the fighting and expenses." "If I am to go to war," argued Elizabeth, "I cannot marry your brother; for my subjects will say that I am dragged into it by my husband, and they will grudge the expense. Suppose, instead of a marriage, we have an alliance not binding me to open war; then I will furnish you with money *underhand*. You know you have got to fight. You cannot afford to let Philip go on increasing his power."

Henry remained doggedly firm. No marriage, no war. At last, finding she could not stir him, Elizabeth again concluded a treaty of marriage, but with the extraordinary proviso that six weeks should be left for private explanations by letter between herself and Alençon. It soon appeared what this meant. In these six weeks Elizabeth furnished her suitor with money, and incited him to make a sudden attack on Parma, who was then besieging Cambray, close to the French frontier. Alençon, thinking himself now sure of the marriage, collected 15,000 men; and Henry, though not openly assisting him, no longer prohibited the enterprise. But, as soon as Elizabeth thought they were sufficiently committed, she gave them to understand that the marriage must be again deferred, that her subjects were discontented, that she could only join in a defensive alliance, but that she would furnish money "in reasonable sort" *underhand*.

All this is very unscrupulous, very shameless, even for that shameless age. Hardened liars like Henry and Alençon thought it too bad. *They* were ready for violence as well as fraud, and availed themselves of whichever method came handiest. Elizabeth also used the weapon which nature had given her. Being constitutionally averse from any but peaceful methods, she made up for it by a double dose of fraud. *Dente lupus, cornu taurus.* It would have been useless for a male statesman to try to pass himself off as a fickle impulsive, susceptible being, swayed from one moment to another in his political schemes by passions and weaknesses that are thought natural in the other sex. This was Elizabeth's advantage, and she made the most of it. She was a masculine woman simulating, when it suited her purpose, a feminine character. The men against whom she was matched were never sure whether they were dealing with a crafty and determined politician, or a vain, flighty, amorous woman. This uncertainty was constantly putting them out in their calculations. Alençon would never have been so taken in if he had not told himself that any folly might be expected from an elderly woman enamoured of a young man.

On this occasion Elizabeth scored, if not the full success she had hoped from her audacious mystification, yet no inconsiderable portion of it. Henry managed to draw back just in time, and was not let in for a big war. But Alençon, at the head of 15,000 men, and close to Cambray, could not for very shame beat a retreat. Parma retired at his approach, and the French army entered Cambray in triumph (August 1581). Alençon therefore had been put in harness to some purpose.

Though Henry III. had good reason to complain of the way he had been treated, he did not make it a quarrel with Elizabeth. His interests, as she saw all along, were too closely bound up with hers to permit him to think of such a thing. On the contrary, he renewed the alliance of 1572 in an ampler form, though it still remained strictly defensive. Alençon, after relieving and victualling Cambray, disbanded his army, and went over to England again to press for the marriage (Nov. 1581). Thither he was followed by ambassadors from the States. By the advice of Orange they had resolved to take him as their sovereign, and they were now urgently pressing him to return to the Netherlands to be installed. Elizabeth added her pressure; but he was unwilling to leave England until he should have secured the marriage. For three months (Nov. 1581 —Feb. 1582) did Elizabeth try every art to make him accept promise for performance. She was thoroughly in her element. To win her game in this way, not by the brutal arbitrament of war, or even by the ordinary tricks of vicarious diplomacy, but by artifices personally executed, feats of cajolery that might seem improbable on the stage,—this was delightful in the highest degree. The more distrustful Alençon showed himself, the keener was the pleasure of handling him. One day he is hidden behind a curtain to view her elegant dancing; not, surely, that he might be smitten with it, but that he might think she desired him to be smitten. Another day she kisses him on the lips (*en la boca*) in the presence of the French ambassador. She gives him a ring. She presents him to her household as their future master. She orders the Bishop of Lincoln to draw up a marriage service. It is a repulsive spectacle; but, after all, we are not so much disgusted with the elderly woman who pretends to be willing to marry the young man, as with the young man who is really willing to marry the elderly woman. Unfortunately for Elizabeth, her acting was so realistic that it not only took in contemporaries, but has persuaded many modern writers that she was really influenced by a degrading passion.

Henry III. himself was at last induced to believe that Elizabeth was this time in earnest. But he could not be driven from his determination to risk nothing till he saw the marriage actually concluded. Pinart, the French Secretary of State, was accordingly sent over to settle the terms. Elizabeth demanded one concession after another, and finally asked for the restitution of Calais. There was no mistaking what this meant. Pinart, in the King's name, formally forbade Alençon to proceed to the Netherlands except as a married man, and tried to intimidate Elizabeth by threatening that his master would ally himself with Philip. But she laughed at him, and told him that *she* could have the Spanish alliance whenever she chose, which was perfectly true. Alençon himself gave way. He felt that he was being played with. He had come over here, with a *fatuité* not uncommon among young Frenchmen, expecting to bend a love-sick Queen to serve his political designs. He found himself, to his intense mortification, bent to serve hers. Ashamed to show his face in France without either his Belgian dominions or his English wife, he was fain to accept Elizabeth's solemn promise that she would marry him as soon as she could, and allowed himself to be shipped off under the escort of an English fleet to the Netherlands (Feb. 1582).

According to Mr. Froude, "the Prince of Orange

intimated that Alençon was accepted by the States only as a pledge that England would support them; if England failed them, they would not trust their fortunes to so vain an idiot." This statement appears to be drawn from the second-hand tattle of Mendoza, and is probably, like much else from that source, unworthy of credit. But whether Orange sent such an "intimation" or not, it cannot be allowed to weigh against the ample evidence that Alençon was accepted by him and by the States mainly for the sake of the French forces he could raise on his own account, and the assistance which he undertook to procure from his brother. Neither Orange nor any one else regarded him as an idiot. Orange had not been led to expect that he would bring any help from England except money supplied underhand; and money Elizabeth did furnish in very considerable quantities. But the Netherlanders now expected everything to be done for them, and were backward with their contributions both in men and money. Clearly there is something to be said for the let-alone policy to which Elizabeth usually leant.

The States intended Alençon's sovereignty to be of the strictly constitutional kind, such as it had been before the encroachments of Philip and his father. This did not suit the young Frenchman, and at the beginning of 1583 he attempted a *coup-d'état*, not without encouragement from some of the Belgian Catholics. At Antwerp his French troops were defeated with great bloodshed by the citizens, and the general voice of the country was for sending him about his business. But both Elizabeth and Orange, though disconcerted and disgusted by his treachery, still saw nothing better to be done than to patch up the breach and retain his services. Both of them urged this course on the States—Orange with his usual dignified frankness; Elizabeth in the crooked, blustering fashion which has brought upon her policy, in so many instances, reproach which it does not really deserve. Norris, the commander of the English volunteers, had discountenanced the *coup-d'état* and taken his orders from the States. Openly Elizabeth reprimanded him, and ordered him to bring his men back to England. Secretly she told him he had done well, and bade him remain where he was. Norris was in fact there to protect the interests of England quite as much against the French as against Spain. There is not the least ground for the assertion that in promoting a reconciliation with Alençon, Orange acted under pressure from Elizabeth. Everything goes to show that he, the wisest and noblest statesman of his time, thought it the only course open to the States, unless they were prepared to submit to Philip. Both Elizabeth and Orange felt that the first necessity was to keep the quarrel alive between the Frenchman and the Spaniard. The English Queen therefore continued to feed Alençon with hopes of marriage, and the States patched up a reconciliation with him (March 1583). But his heart failed him. He saw Parma taking town after town. He knew that he had made himself odious to the Netherlanders. He was covered with shame. He was fatally stricken with consumption. In June 1583 he left Belgium never to return. Within a twelvemonth he was dead.

CHAPTER VII

THE PAPAL ATTACK: 1570-1583

SOVEREIGNS and statesmen in the sixteenth century are to be honoured or condemned according to the degree in which they aimed on the one hand at preserving political order, and on the other at allowing freedom of opinion. It was not always easy to reconcile these two aims. The first was a temporary necessity, and yet was the more urgent—as indeed is always the case with the tasks of the statesman. He is responsible for the present; it is not for him to attempt to provide for a remote future. Political order and the material well-being of nations may be disastrously impaired by the imprudence or weakness of a ruler. Thought, after all, may be trusted to take care of itself in the long-run.

To the modern Liberal, with his doctrine of absolute religious equality, toleration seems an insult, and anything short of toleration is regarded as persecution. In the sixteenth century the most advanced statesmen did not see their way to proclaim freedom of public worship and of religious discussion. It was much if they tolerated freedom of opinion, and connived at a quiet, private propagation of other religions than those established by law. It would be wrong to condemn and despise them as actuated by superstition and narrow-minded prejudice. Their motives were mainly political, and it is reasonable to suppose that they knew better than we do whether a larger toleration was compatible with public order.

We have seen that under the Act of Supremacy, in the first year of Elizabeth, the oath was only tendered to persons holding office, spiritual or temporal, under the crown, and that the penalty for refusing it was only deprivation. But in her fifth year (1563), it was enacted that the oath might be tendered to members of the House of Commons, schoolmasters, and attorneys, who, if they refused it, might be punished by forfeiture of property and perpetual imprisonment. To those who had held any ecclesiastical office, or who should openly disapprove of the established worship, or celebrate or hear mass, the oath might be tendered a second time, with the penalties of high treason for refusal.

That this law authorised an atrocious persecution cannot be disputed, and there is no doubt that many zealous Protestants wished it to be enforced. But the practical question is, Was it enforced? The government wished to be armed with the power of using it, and for the purpose of expelling Catholics from offices it was extensively used. But no one was at this time visited with the severer penalties, the bishops having been privately forbidden to tender the oath a second time to any one without special instructions.

The Act of Uniformity, passed in the first year of

Elizabeth, prohibited the use of any but the established liturgy, whether in public or private, under pain of perpetual imprisonment for the third offence, and imposed a fine of one shilling on recusants—that is, upon persons who absented themselves from church on Sundays and holidays. To what extent Catholics were interfered with under this Act has been a matter of much dispute. Most of them, during the first eleven years of Elizabeth, either from ignorance or worldliness, treated the Anglican service as equivalent to the Catholic, and made no difficulty about attending church, even after this compliance with the law had been forbidden by Pius IV. in the sixth year of Elizabeth. Only the more scrupulous absented themselves, and called in the ministrations of the "old priests," who with more or less secrecy said mass in private houses. Some of these offenders were certainly punished before Elizabeth had been two years on the throne. The enforcement of laws was by no means so uniform in those days as it is now. Much depended on the leanings of the noblemen and justices of the peace in different localities. Both from disposition and policy Elizabeth desired, as a general rule, to connive at Catholic nonconformity when it did not take an aggressive and fanatical form. But she had no scruple about applying the penalties of these Acts to individuals who for any reason, religious or political, were specially obnoxious to her.

So things went on till the northern insurrection: the laws authorising a searching and sanguinary persecution; the Government, much to the disgust of zealous Protestants, declining to put those laws in execution. Judged by modern ideas, the position of the Catholics was intolerable; but if measured by the principles of government then universally accepted, or if compared with the treatment of persons ever so slightly suspected of heresy in countries cursed with the Inquisition, it was not a position of which they had any great reason to complain; nor did the large majority of them complain.

Pope Pius IV. (1559-1566) was comparatively cautious and circumspect in his attitude towards Elizabeth. But his successor Pius V. (1566-1572), having made up his mind that her destruction was the one thing necessary for the defeat of heresy in Europe, strove to stir up against her rebellion at home and invasion from abroad. A bull deposing her, and absolving her subjects from their allegiance, was drawn up. But while Pius, conscious of the offence which it would give to all the sovereigns of Europe, delayed to issue it, the northern rebellion flared up and was trampled out. The absence of such a bull was by many Catholics made an excuse for holding aloof from the rebel earls. When it was too late the bull was issued (Feb. 1570). Philip and Charles IX.—sovereigns first and Catholics afterwards—refused to let it be published in their dominions.

After the northern insurrection the Queen issued a remarkable appeal to her people, which was ordered to be placarded in every parish, and read in every church. She could point with honest pride to eleven years of such peace abroad and tranquillity at home as no living Englishman could remember. Her economy had enabled her to conduct the government without any of the illegal exactions to which former sovereigns had resorted. "She had never sought the life, the blood, the goods, the houses, estates or lands of any person in her dominions." This happy state of things the rebels had tried to disturb on pretext of religion. They had no real grievance on that score. Attendance at parish church was indeed obligatory by law, though, she might have added, it was very loosely enforced. But she disclaimed any wish to pry into opinions, or to inquire in what sense any one understood rites or ceremonies. In other words, the language of the communion service was not incompatible with the doctrine of transubstantiation, and loyal Catholics were at liberty, were almost invited, to interpret it in that sense if they liked.

This compromise between their religious and political obligations had in fact been hitherto adopted by the large majority of English Catholics. But a time was come when it was to be no longer possible for them. They were summoned to make their choice between their duty as citizens and their duty as Catholics. The summons had come, not from the Queen, but from the Pope, and it is not strange that they had thenceforth a harder time of it. Many of them, indignant with the Pope for bringing trouble upon them, gave up the struggle and conformed to the Established Church. The temper of the rest became more bitter and dangerous. The Puritan Parliament of 1571 passed a bill to compel all persons not only to attend church, but to receive the communion twice a year; and another making formal reconciliation to the Church of Rome high treason both for the convert and the priest who should receive him. Here we have the persecuting spirit, which was as inherent in the zealous Protestant as in the zealous Catholic. Attempts to excuse such legislation, as prompted by political reasons, can only move the disgust of every honest-minded man. The first of these bills did not receive the royal assent, though Cecil—just made Lord Burghley—had strenuously pushed it through the Upper House. Elizabeth probably saw that its only effect would be to enable the Protestant zealots in every parish to enjoy the luxury of harassing their quiet Catholic neighbours, who attended church but would scruple to take the sacrament.

The Protestant spirit of this House of Commons showed itself not only in laws for strengthening the Government and persecuting the Catholics, but in attempts to puritanise the Prayer-book, which much displeased the Queen. Strickland, one of the Puritan leaders, was forbidden to attend the House. But such was the irritation caused by this invasion of its privileges, that the prohibition was removed after one day. It was in this session of Parliament that the doctrines of the Church of England were finally determined by the imposition on the clergy of the Thirty-nine Articles, which, as every one knows, are much more Protestant than the Prayer-book. Till then they had only had the sanction of Convocation.

During the first forty years or so, from the beginning of the Reformation, Protestantism spread in most parts of Europe with great rapidity. It was not merely an intellectual revolt against doctrines no longer credible. The numbers of the reformers were swelled, and their force intensified by the flocking in of pious souls, athirst for personal holiness, and of many others who, without being high-wrought enthusiasts, were by nature disposed to value whatever seemed to make for a purer morality. The religion which had nurtured Bernard and À Kempis was deserted, not merely as being untrue, but as incompatible with the highest spiritual life—nay, as positively corrupting to society. This imagination, of course, had but a short day. The return to the Bible and the doctrines of primitive Christianity, the deliverance from "the Bishop of Rome and his detestable enormities," were not found to be followed by any general improvement of morals in Protestant countries. He that was unjust was unjust still; he that was filthy was filthy still. The repulsive contrast too often seen between sanctimonious professions and unscrupulous conduct contributed to the disenchantment.

In the meanwhile a great regeneration was going on within the Catholic Church itself. Signs of this can be detected quite as early as the first rise of Protestantism. It is, therefore, not to be attributed to Protestant teaching and example, though doubtless the rivalry of the younger religion stimulated the best energies of the older. No long time elapsed before this regeneration had worked its way to the highest places in the Church. The Popes by whom Elizabeth was confronted were all men of pure lives and single-hearted devotion to the Catholic cause.

The last two years of the Council of Trent (1562-3) were the starting-point of the modern Catholic Church. Many proposals had been made for compromise with

Protestantism. But the Fathers of Trent saw that the only chance of survival for a Church claiming to be Catholic was to remain on the old lines. By the canons and decrees of the Council, ratified by Pius IV., the old doctrines and discipline were confirmed and definitely formulated. One branch indeed of the Papal power was irretrievably gone. Royal authority had become absolute, and the kings, including Philip II., refused to tolerate any interference with it. The Papacy had to acquiesce in the loss of its power over sovereigns. But as regards the bishops and clergy, and things strictly appertaining to religion, its spiritual autocracy, which the great councils of the last century had aimed at breaking, was re-established, and has continued. The new situation, though it seemed to place the Popes on a humbler footing than in the days of Gregory VII. or Innocent III., was a healthy one. It confined them to their spiritual domain, and drove them to make the best of it.

Until the decrees of the Council of Trent, the split between Protestants and Catholics was not definitely and irrevocably decided. Many on both sides had shrunk from admitting it. The Catholic world might seem to be narrowed by the defection of the Protestant States. But all the more clearly did it appear that a Church claiming to be universal is not concerned with political boundaries. The resistance to the spread of heresy had hitherto consisted of many local struggles, in which the repressive measures had emanated from the orthodox sovereigns, and had therefore been fitful and unconnected. But not long after the Tridentine reorganisation, the Pope appears again as commander-in-chief of the Catholic forces, surveying and directing combined operations from one end of Europe to the other. Pius IV. had been with difficulty prevented by Philip from excommunicating Elizabeth. Pius V. had launched his bull, as we have seen, a few months too late (1570); and even then it was not allowed to be published in either Spain or France. The life of that Pope was wasted in earnest remonstrances with the Catholic sovereigns for not executing the sentence of the Church against the heretic Queen. Gregory XIII., who succeeded him just before the Bartholomew Massacre, took the attack into his own hands. He was a warm patron of the Jesuits, who were especially devoted to the centralising system re-established at Trent. He and they had made up their minds that England was the key of the Protestant position; that until Elizabeth was removed no advance was to be hoped for anywhere.

The decline of a religion may be accompanied by a positive increase of earnestness and activity on the part of its remaining votaries, deluding them into a belief that they are but passing through, or have successfully passed through, a period of temporary depression and eclipse. Among the Catholics of the latter part of the sixteenth century there was all the enthusiasm of a religious revival. In no place did this show itself more than at Oxford. There the weak points of popular movements have never been allowed to pass without challenge, and what is really valuable or beautiful in time-worn faiths has been sure of receiving fair-play and something more. The gloss of the Reformation was already worn off. The worldly and carnal were its supporters and directors. It no longer demanded enthusiasm and sacrifice. It walked in purple and fine linen. Young men of quick intellect and high aspirations who, a generation earlier, would have been captivated by its fair promise and have thrown themselves into its current, yielded now to the eternal spell of the older Church, cleansed as she was of her pollutions, and purged of her dross by the discipline of adversity.

The leader of these Oxford enthusiasts was a young fellow of Oriel, William Allen. In the third year of Elizabeth, at the age of twenty-eight, he resigned the Principalship of St. Mary Hall. The next eight years were spent partly abroad, partly in secret missionary work in England, carried on at the peril of his life. The old priests, who with more or less concealment and danger continued to exercise their office among the English Catholics, were gradually dying off. In order to train successors to them, Allen founded an English seminary at Douai (1568). To this important step it was mainly due that the Catholic religion did not become extinct in this country. In the first five years of its existence the college at Douai sent nearly a hundred priests to England.

It was the aim of Allen to put an end to the practical toleration allowed to Catholic laymen of the quieter sort. The Catholic who began by putting in the compulsory number of attendances at his parish church was likely to end by giving up his faith altogether. If he did not, his son would. Allen deliberately preferred a sweeping persecution—one that would make the position of Catholics intolerable, and ripen them for rebellion. He wanted martyrs. The ardent young men whom he trained at Douai and (after 1578) at Rheims, went back to their native land with the clear understanding that of all the services they could render to the Church the greatest would be to die under the hangman's knife.

Gregory XIII. hoped great things from Allen's seminary, and furnished funds for its support. In 1579 Allen went to Rome, and enlisted the support of Mercurian, General of the Jesuits. Two English Jesuits, Robert Parsons and Edward Campion, ex-fellows of Balliol and St. John's, were selected as missionaries. Campion was eight years younger than Allen. He had had a brilliant career at Oxford, being especially distinguished for his eloquence. He was at that time personally known to both Cecil and the Queen, and enjoyed their favour. He took deacon's orders in 1568, but not long afterwards joined Allen at Douai, and formally abjured the Anglican Church. He had been six years a Jesuit when he was despatched on his dangerous mission to England.

Tired of waiting for the initiative of Philip, Gregory XIII. and the Jesuits had planned a threefold attack on Elizabeth in England, Scotland, and Ireland. In England a revivalist movement was to be carried on among the Catholics by the missionaries. Catholic writers have been at great pains to argue that this was a purely religious movement, prosecuted with the single object of saving souls. The Jesuits have always known their men and employed them with discrimination. Saving of souls was very likely the simple object of a man of Campion's saintly and exalted nature. He himself declared that he had been strictly forbidden to meddle with worldly concerns or affairs of State, and nothing inconsistent with this declaration was proved against him at his trial. But without laying any stress on statements extracted from prisoners under torture, we cannot doubt that his employers aimed at re-establishing Catholicism in England by rebellion and foreign invasion. This was thoroughly understood by every missionary who crossed the sea; and if Campion never alluded to it even in his most familiar conversations he must have had an extraordinary control over his tongue.

The evidence that the assassination of the Queen was a recognised part of the Jesuit plan, determined by the master spirits and accepted by all the subordinate agents, is perhaps not quite conclusive. If proved, it would only show that they were not more scrupulous than most statesmen and politicians of the time. Lax as sixteenth century notions were about political murder, there were always some consciences more tender than others. It is likely enough that Campion personally disapproved of such projects, and that they were not thrust upon his attention. But he can hardly have avoided being aware that they were contemplated by the less squeamish of his brethren.

Campion and Parsons came to England in disguise in the summer of 1580. Their mission was not a success. It only served to show how much more securely Elizabeth was seated on her throne than in the earlier years of her reign. In his letters to Rome, Campion boasts of the welcome he met with everywhere, the crowds that attended his preaching, the ardour of the Catholics, and the disrepute into which Protestantism was falling. He had evidently worked himself up to such a state of ecstasy that he was living in a world of his own imagination, and was no competent witness of facts. He crept about England in various disguises, and when he was in districts where the nobles and gentry favoured the old religion, he preached with a publicity which seems extraordinary to us in these days when the laws are executed with prompt uniformity by means of railways, telegraphs, and a well-organised police. In the sixteenth century England had nothing that can be called an organised machinery for the prevention and detection of crime. If an outbreak occurred the Government collected militia, and trampled it out with an energy that took no account of law and feared no consequences. But in ordinary times it had to depend on the local justices of the peace and parish constables, and if they were remiss the laws were a dead letter. There were no newspapers. The high-roads were few and bad. One parish did not know what was going on in the next. Campion could be passed on from one gentleman's house to another on horses quite as good as any officer of the Government rode, and could travel all over England without ever using a high-road or showing his face in a town. If he preached to a hundred people in some Lancashire village, Lord Derby did not want to know it, and before the news reached Burghley or Walsingham he would be in another county, or perhaps back in London—then, as now, the safest of all hiding-places. Thus, though a warrant was issued for his arrest as soon as he arrived in

England, it was not till July in the next year (1581) that he was taken, after an unusually public and protracted appearance in the neighbourhood of Oxford.

He had little or nothing to show for his twelve months' tour, and this although the Government had, as Allen hoped, allowed itself to be provoked into an increase of severity which seems to have been quite unnecessary. The large majority of Catholic laymen would evidently have preferred that both Seminarists and Jesuits should keep away. They did not want civil war. They did not want to be persecuted. They were against a foreign invasion, without which they knew very well that Elizabeth could not be deposed. They were even loyal to her. They were content to wait till she should disappear in the course of nature and make room for the Queen of Scots. Mendoza writes to Philip that "they place themselves in the hands of God, and are willing to sacrifice life and all in the service, *but scarcely with that burning zeal which they ought to show.*"

By the bull of Pius V., Englishmen were forbidden to acknowledge Elizabeth as their Queen; in other words, they were ordered to expose themselves to the penalties of treason. If the Pope would be satisfied with nothing less than this, it was quite certain that he would alienate most of his followers in England. Gregory XIII. therefore had authorised the Jesuits to explain that although the Protestants, by *willingly* acknowledging the Queen, were incurring the damnation pronounced by the bull, Catholics would be excused for *unwillingly* acknowledging her until some opportunity arrived for dethroning her. Protestant writers have exclaimed against this distinction as treacherous. It was perfectly reasonable. It represents, for instance, the attitude of every Alsatian who accords an unwilling recognition to the German Emperor. But the English Government intolerantly and unwisely made it the occasion for harassing the consciences of men who were most of them guiltless of any intention to rebel.

Amongst other persecuting laws passed early in 1581, was one which raised the fine for non-attendance at church to twenty pounds a month. Such a measure was calculated to excite much more wide-spread disaffection than the hanging of a few priests. It was not intended to be a *brutum fulmen*. The names of all recusants in each parish were returned to the Council. They amounted to about 50,000, and the fines exacted became a not inconsiderable item in the royal revenue. That number certainly formed but a small portion of the Catholic population. But if all the rest had been in the habit of going to church, contrary to the Pope's express injunction, rather than pay a small fine, the Government ought to have seen that they were not the stuff of which rebels are made.

Campion, after being compelled by torture to disclose the names of his hosts in different counties, was called on to maintain the Catholic doctrines in a three days' discussion before a large audience against four Protestant divines, who do not seem to have been ashamed of themselves. He was offered pardon if he would attend once in church. As he steadfastly refused, he was racked again till his limbs were dislocated. When he had partially recovered he was put on his trial, along with several of his companions, not under any of the recent anti-catholic laws but under the ordinary statute of Edward III., for " compassing and imagining the Queen's death "—such a horror had the Burghleys and Walsinghams of anything like religious persecution! Being unable to hold up his hand to plead Not Guilty, " two of his companions raised it for him, first kissing the broken joints." According to Mendoza (whom on other occasions we are invited to accept as a witness of truth), his nails had been torn from his fingers. Apart from his religious belief nothing treasonable was proved against him in deed or word. He acknowledged Elizabeth for his rightful sovereign, as the new interpretation of the papal bull permitted him to do, but he declined to give any opinion about the Pope's right to depose princes. This was enough for the judge and jury, and he was found guilty. At the place of execution he was again offered his pardon if he would deny the papal right of deposition, or even hear a Protestant sermon. He wished the Queen a long and quiet reign and all prosperity, but more he would not say. At the quartering "a drop of blood spirted on the clothes of a youth named Henry Walpole, to whom it came as a divine command. Walpole, converted on the spot, became a Jesuit, and soon after met the same fate on the same spot."

Mr. Froude's comment is that "if it be lawful in defence of national independence to kill open enemies in war, it is more lawful to execute the secret conspirator who is teaching doctrines in the name of God which are certain to be fatal to it." It would perhaps be enough to remark that this reasoning amply justifies some of the worst atrocities of the French Revolution. Hallam and Macaulay have condemned it by anticipation in language which will commend itself to all who are not swayed by religious, or, what is more offensive, anti-religious bigotry.[1]

Cruel as the English criminal law was, and long remained, it never authorised the use of torture to extract confession. The rack in the Tower is said to have made its appearance, with other innovations of absolute government, in the reign of Edward IV. But it seems to have been little used before the reign of Elizabeth, under whom it became the ordinary preliminary to a political trial. For this the chief blame must rest personally on Burghley. Opinions may differ as to his rank as a statesman, but no one will contest his eminent talents as a minister of police. In the former capacity he had sufficient sense of shame to publish a Pecksniffian apology for his employment of the rack. "None," he says, "of those who were at any time put to the rack were asked, during their torture, any question as to points of doctrine, but merely concerning their plots and conspiracies, and the persons with whom they had dealings, and *what was their own opinion* as to the Pope's right to deprive the Queen of her crown." What was this but a point of doctrine? The wretched victim who conscientiously believed it (as all Christendom once did), but wished to save himself by silence, was driven either to tell a lie or to consign himself to rope and knife. "The Queen's servants, the warders, whose office and act it

[1] Hallam, *Constitutional History*, Chapter III. Macaulay, *Essay on Hallam's Constitutional History*.

is to handle the rack, were ever, by those that attended the examinations, specially charged to use it in so charitable a manner as such a thing might be." It may be hoped that there are not many who would dissent from Hallam's remark that "such miserable excuses serve only to mingle contempt with our detestation." He adds: "It is due to Elizabeth to observe that she ordered the torture to be disused." I do not know what authority there is for this statement. Three years later the Protestant Archbishop of Dublin was puzzled how to torture the Catholic Archbishop of Cashel, because there was no "rack or other engine" in Dublin. Walsingham, on being consulted, suggested that his feet might be toasted against the fire, which was accordingly done. Some of the Anglican bishops, as might be expected from fanatics, were forward in recommending torture. But Cecil was no more of a fanatic than his mistress. What both of them cared for was not a particular religious belief—they had both of them conformed to Popery under Queen Mary—but the sovereign's claim to prescribe religious belief, or rather religious profession, and they were provoked with the missionaries for thwarting them. Provoking it was, no doubt. But everything seems to show that it would have been better to pursue the earlier policy of the reign; to be content with enacting severe laws which practically were not put into execution.

The English branch of the Jesuit attack was, for political purposes, a dead failure. A few persons of rank, who at heart were Catholics before, were formally reconciled to the Pope. Mendoza claims that

K

among them were six peers whose names he conceals. These peers, if he is to be believed, were treasonable enough in their designs. But, even by his account, they were determined not to stir unless a foreign army should have first entered England.

How far Mendoza's master was from seeing his way to attack England at this time was strikingly shown by his behaviour under the most audacious outrage that Elizabeth had yet inflicted on him. Some twelve months before (October 1580), Drake had returned from his famous voyage round the world. That voyage was nothing else than a piratical expedition, for which it was notorious that the funds had been mainly furnished by Elizabeth and Leicester. On sea and land Drake had robbed Philip of gold, silver, and precious stones to the value of at least £750,000. In vain did Mendoza clamour for restitution and talk about war. Elizabeth kept the booty, knighted Drake, and openly showed him every mark of confidence and favour. When Mendoza told her that as she would not hear words, they must come to cannon and see if she would hear them, she replied ("quietly in her most natural voice") that, if he used threats of that kind, she would throw him into prison. The correspondence between the Spanish ambassador and his master shows that, however big they might talk about cannon, they felt themselves paralysed by Elizabeth's intimate relations with France. She had managed to keep free from any offensive alliance with Henry III. But at the first sound of the Spanish cannon she could have it. She was, therefore, secure. Probably the whole history of diplomacy does not show another instance of such a complicated balance of forces so dexterously manipulated.

The Irish branch of the Papal attack, the landing of the legate Sanders, the insurrection of Desmond (1579-1583), the massacre of the Pope's Italian soldiers at Smerwick (1580), must be passed over here. It is enough to say that, in Ireland, too, the Catholics were beaten. We turn now to their attempt to get hold of Scotland (1579-1582).

Scotland was in a state of anarchy, from which it could only be rescued by an able and courageous king. The nobles, instead of becoming weaker, as elsewhere, had acquired a strength and independence greater even than their fathers had enjoyed. Thirty years earlier, the Church had possessed quite half the land of the country, and had steadily supported the crown. Almost the whole of this wealth had been seized in one form or another by the nobles. And though, as compared with English noblemen, they were still poor in money, they were much bigger men relatively to their sovereign. The power of the crown was extensive enough in theory. What was wanted was a king who should know how to convert it into a reality. That was more than any regent could do. Even Moray had not succeeded. The house of Douglas was one of the most powerful in Scotland, and Morton, who had been looked on as its head during the minority of the Earl of Angus, was an able and daring man. But he had not the large views, the public spirit, or the integrity of Moray. He was feared by all, hated by many, respected by none. As a mere party chief, no one would have been better able to hold his own. As representing the crown, he had every man's hand against him. To subsidise such a man was perfectly useless. If Elizabeth was to make his cause her own, she might just as well undertake the conquest of Scotland at once.

The essence of the good understanding between England and France was that both countries should keep their hands off Scotland. Elizabeth, knowing that if worst came to worst, she could always be beforehand with France in the northern kingdom, could afford to respect this arrangement, and she did mean to respect it. France, on the other hand, being also well aware of the advantage given to England by geographical situation, was always tempted to steal a march on her, and even when most desirous of her alliance, never quite gave up intrigues in Scotland. This was equally the case whatever party was uppermost at the French court, whether its policy was being directed by the King or by the Duke of Guise.

The Jesuits looked on Guise as their fighting man, who was to do the work which they could not prevail on crowned heads to undertake. James, though only thirteen, had been declared of age. It was too late to think of deposing him. If his character was feeble, his understanding and acquirements were much beyond his years, and his preferences were already a force to be reckoned with in Scotch politics. His interests were evidently opposed to those of his mother. But the Jesuits hoped to persuade him that his seat would never be secure unless he came to a compromise with her on the terms that he was to accept the crown as her gift and recognise her joint-sovereignty. This

would throw him entirely into the hands of the
Catholic nobles, and would be a virtual declaration
of war against Elizabeth. He would have to proclaim himself a Catholic, and call in the French. It
was hoped that Philip, jealous though he had always
been of French interference, would not object to an
expedition warranted by the Jesuits and commanded
by Guise, who was more and more sinking into a tool
of Spain and Rome. A combined army of Scotch and
French would pour across the Border. It would be
joined by the English Catholics. Elizabeth would be
deposed, and Mary set on the throne.

It was a pretty scheme on paper, but certain to
break down in every stage of its execution. James
might chaffer with his mother; but, young as he
was, he knew well that she meant to overreach him.
He would be glad enough to get rid of Morton, but
he did not want to be a puppet in the hands of the
Marians. He did not like the Presbyterian preachers;
but the young pedant already valued himself on his
skill in confuting the apologists of Popery. He resented Elizabeth's lectures; but he knew that his
succession to the English crown depended on her good
will, and he meant to keep on good terms with her.
No approval of the scheme could be obtained from
Philip, and if he did not peremptorily forbid the
expedition, it was because he did not believe it would
come off. If a French army had appeared in Scotland, it would have been treated as all foreigners
were in that country. And finally, if, *per impossibile*,
the French and Scotch had entered England, they
would have been overwhelmed by such an unanimous

uprising of the English people of all parties and creeds as had never been witnessed in our history.

Historians, who would have us believe that Elizabeth was constantly bringing England to the verge of ruin by her stinginess and want of spirit, represent this combination as highly formidable. It required careful watching; but the only thing that could make it really dangerous was rash and premature employment of force by England—the course advocated not only by Burghley, but by the whole Council. Elizabeth seems to have stood absolutely alone in her opinion; but here, as always, though she allowed her ministers to speak their minds freely, she did not fear to act on her own judgment against their unanimous advice.

To carry out their schemes, Guise and the Jesuits sent to Scotland a nephew of the late Regent Lennox, Esmé Stuart, who had been brought up in France, and bore the title of Count d'Aubigny (September 1579). He speedily won the heart of the King, who created him Earl, and afterwards Duke of Lennox. Elizabeth soon obtained proof of his designs, and urged Morton to resist them by force. But the favourite, professing to be converted to Protestantism, enlisted the preachers on his side, and, by this unnatural coalition, Morton was brought to the scaffold (June 1581). During the interval between his arrest and execution, the English Council were urgent with Elizabeth to invade Scotland, rescue the Anglophile leader, and crush Lennox. She went all lengths in the way of threats. Lord Hunsdon was even ordered to muster an army on the Border. But this last step at once produced an energetic protest from the French ambassador; and in Scotland there was a general rally of all parties against the "auld enemies." Elizabeth had never meant to make her threats good, and Morton was left to his fate. She was quite right not to invade Scotland; but, that being her intention, she should not have tempted Morton to treason by the promise of her protection. No male statesman would have been so insensible to dishonour.

The death of the man who, next to Moray, had been the mainstay of the Reformation and the scourge of the Marian party, was received with a shout of exultation from Catholic Europe. Already in their heated imaginations the Jesuits saw the Kirk overthrown and the vantage ground gained for an attack on England. Some modern historians—with less excuse, since they have the sequel before their eyes —make the same blunder. The situation was really unchanged. Morton, who had the true antipathy of a Scottish noble to clerics of all sorts, had plundered the Kirk ministers, and tried to bring them under the episcopal yoke. He had quarrelled with most of his old associates of the Congregation. It was their enmity quite as much as the attack of Lennox that had pulled him down. When he was out of the way they naturally reverted to an Anglophile policy. The weakness of the Catholic party was plainly shown by the fact that Lennox himself, the pupil of the Jesuits, never ventured to throw off the disguise of a heretic.

The further development of the Jesuit scheme met with difficulties on all sides. Most even of the

Catholic lords were alarmed by the suggestion that James should hold the crown by the gift of his mother, because it would imply that hitherto he had not been lawful King; and this would invalidate their titles to all the lands they had grabbed from Church and crown during the last fourteen years. It would seem therefore that, if they had harassed the Government during all that time, it was from a liking for anarchy rather than from attachment to Mary. Two Jesuits, Crichton and Holt, who were sent in disguise to Scotland, found Lennox desponding. He was obliged to confess that, greatly as he had fascinated the King, he could not move him an inch in his religious opinions. On the contrary, James imagined that his controversial skill had converted Lennox, and was extremely proud of the feat. The only course remaining was to seize him, and send him to France or Spain, Lennox in the meantime administering the Government in the name of Mary. But to carry out this stroke, Lennox said he must have a foreign army. In view of the mutual jealousy of France and Spain it was suggested that, if Philip would furnish money underhand, the Pope might send an Italian army direct to Scotland, *viâ* the Straits of Gibraltar. Crichton went to Rome to arrange this precious scheme, and Holt was proceeding to Madrid. But Philip forbade him to come. If Lennox could convert James, or send him to Spain, well and good. But until one of these preliminaries was accomplished he was to expect no help from Philip. Nor were prospects more hopeful on the side of France. Mary from her prison implored Guise to undertake the long-planned expedition. But he would not venture it without the assent of his own sovereign and the King of Spain. While he was hesitating, the Anglophiles patched up their differences and got possession of the King's person (Raid of Ruthven, August 1582). His tears were unavailing. "Better bairns greet," said the Master of Glamis, "than bearded men." The favourite fled to France, where he died in the next year.

Thus once more had it been clearly shown that if the Anglophiles were left to depend on themselves they would not fail to do all that was necessary to safeguard English interests. "Anglophiles" is a convenient appellation. But, strictly speaking, there was no party in Scotland that loved England. There was a religious party to whom it was of the highest importance that Elizabeth should be safe and powerful. She was therefore certain of its co-operation. This party would not be always uppermost; for Scottish nobles were too selfish, too treacherous, too much interested in disorder to permit any stability. But, whether in power or in opposition, it would be able and it would be obliged to serve English interests. There was only one way in which it could be paralysed or alienated, and that was by a recurrence on the part of England to the traditions of armed interference inherited by Elizabeth's councillors from Henry VIII. and the Protector Somerset.

Such is the plain history of this Jesuit and Papal scheme which we are asked to believe was so dangerous to England and so inadequately handled by Elizabeth. She had not shown much concern for her honour. But her coolness, her intrepidity, her correct estimate of the forces with which she had to deal, her magnificent confidence in her own judgment, saved England from the endless expenditure of blood and treasure into which her advisers would have plunged, and prolonged the formal peace with her three principal neighbours, a peace of already unexampled duration, and of incalculable advantage to her country.

The policy which Elizabeth had thus deliberately adopted towards Scotland she persisted in. The successful Anglophiles clamoured for pensions, and her ministers were for gratifying them. She was willing to give a moderate pension to James, but not a penny to the nobles. "Her servants and favourites," she said, "professed to love her for her high qualities, Alençon for her beauty, and the Scots for her crown; but they all wanted the same thing in the end; they wanted nothing but her money, and they should not have it." She had ascertained that James regarded his mother as his rival for the crowns of both kingdoms, and that, whatever he might sometimes pretend, his real wish was that she should be kept under lock and key. She had also satisfied herself that the Scottish noblemen on whom Mary counted would, with very few exceptions, throw every difficulty in the way of her restoration, out of regard for their own private interests—the only *datum* from which it was safe to calculate in dealing with a Scottish nobleman. She therefore felt herself secure. By communicating her knowledge to Mary she could show her the hopelessness of her intrigues in Scotland; while a resumption of friendly negotiations for her restoration would always be a cheap and effectual way of intimidating James. Thus she could look on with equanimity when his new favourite Stewart, Earl of Arran,[1] again chased the Anglophiles into England (December 1583). Arran himself urgently entreated her to accept him and his young master as the genuine Anglophiles. Walsingham's voice was still for war. But, with both factions at her feet and suing for her favour, Elizabeth had good reason to be satisfied with her policy of leaving the Scottish nobles to worry it out among themselves.

[1] James had given this man the title and estates of the exiled Hamiltons.

CHAPTER VIII

THE PROTECTORATE OF THE NETHERLANDS: 1584-86

WE are now approaching the great crisis of the reign—
some may think of English history—the grand struggle
with Spain; a struggle which, if Elizabeth had allowed
herself to be guided by her most celebrated counsellors, would have been entered upon a quarter of
a century earlier. England was then unarmed and
weighed down with a load of debt, the legacy of three
thriftless and pugnacious reigns. The population was
still mainly Catholic. The great nobles still thought
themselves a match for the crown, and many of them
longed to make one more effort to assert their old
position in the State. Trade and industry were lan-
guishing. The poorer classes were suffering and discontented. Scotland was in the hands of a most dangerous
enemy, whose title to the English crown was held
by many to be better than Elizabeth's. Philip II.,
as yet unharassed by revolt, seemed almost to have
drawn England as a sort of satellite into the vast orbit
of his empire.

Nearly a generation had now passed away since
Elizabeth ascended the throne. Every year of it had

seen some amendment in the condition of the country. Under a pacific and thrifty Government taxation had been light beyond precedent. All debts, even those of Henry VIII., had been honourably paid off. While the lord of American gold mines and of the richest commercial centres in Europe could not raise a loan on any terms, Elizabeth could borrow when she pleased at five per cent. But she had ceased to borrow, for she had a modest surplus stored in her treasury, a department of the administration managed under her own close personal supervision. A numerous militia had been enrolled and partially trained. Large magazines of arms had been accumulated. A navy had been created; not a large one indeed; but it did not need to be large, for the warship of those days did not differ from the ordinary vessel of commerce, nor was its crew differently trained. The royal navy could therefore be indefinitely increased if need arose. Philip's great generals, Alva and Parma, had long come to the conclusion that the conquest of England would be the most difficult enterprise their master could undertake. The wealth of landed proprietors and traders had increased enormously. New manufactures had been started by exiles from the Netherlands. New branches of foreign commerce had been opened up. The poor were well employed and contented. I believe it would be impossible to find in the previous history of England, or, for that matter, of Europe, since the fall of the Roman Empire, any instance of peace, prosperity, and good government extending over so many years.

Looking abroad we find that in all directions the strength and security of Elizabeth's position had been immensely increased. Her ministers, especially Walsingham—for Burghley in his old age came at last to see more with the eyes of his mistress—believed that by a more spirited policy Scotland might have been converted into a submissive and valuable ally. Elizabeth alone saw that this was impossible; that, so treated, Scotland would become to England what Holland was to Philip, what "the Spanish ulcer" was afterwards to Napoleon—a fatal drain on her strength and resources. It was enough for Elizabeth if the northern kingdom was so handled as to be harmless; and this, as I have shown, was in fact its condition from the moment that the only Scottish ruler who could be really dangerous was locked up in England.

The Dutch revolt crippled Philip. The conquest of England was postponed till the Dutch revolt should be suppressed. Why then, it has been asked, did not Elizabeth support the Dutch more vigorously? The answer is a simple one. If she had done so the suppression of the Dutch revolt would have been postponed to the conquest of England. This is proved by the events now to be related. Elizabeth was obliged by new circumstances to intervene more vigorously in the Netherlands, and the result was the Armada. If the attack had come ten or fifteen years earlier the fortune of England might have been different.

Elizabeth's foreign policy has been judged unfavourably by writers who have failed to keep in view how completely it turned on her relations with France. Though her interests and those of Henry III. cannot be called identical, they coincided sufficiently to make it possible to keep up a good understanding which was of the highest advantage to both countries. But to maintain this good understanding there was need of the coolest temper and judgment on the part of the rulers; for the two peoples were hopelessly hostile. They were like two gamecocks in adjoining pens. The Spaniards were respected and liked by our countrymen. Their grave dignity, even their stiff assumption of intrinsic superiority, were too like our own not to awake a certain appreciative sympathy. Whereas all Englishmen from peer to peasant would at any time have enjoyed a tussle with France, until its burdens began to be felt.

Henry III., with whom the Valois dynasty was about to expire, was far from being the incompetent driveller depicted by most historians. He had good abilities, plenty of natural courage when roused, and a thorough comprehension of the politics of his day. His aims and plans were well conceived. But with no child to care for, and immersed in degrading self-indulgence, he wearied of the exertions and sacrifices necessary for carrying them through. Short spells of sensible and energetic action were succeeded by periods of unworthy lassitude and pusillanimous surrender. Before he came to the throne he had been the chief organiser of the Bartholomew Massacre. As King he naturally inclined, like Elizabeth, William of Orange, and Henry of Navarre, to make considerations of religion subordinate to considerations of State. Both he and Navarre would have been glad to throw over the fanatical or factious partisans by whom they were surrounded, and rally the *Politiques* to their support. But it was a step that neither as yet ventured openly to take. The one was obliged to affect zeal for the old religion, the other for the new.

Elizabeth's ministers, with short-sighted animosity, had been urging her throughout her reign to give vigorous support to the Huguenots. She herself took a broader view of the situation. She preferred to deal with the legitimate government of France recognised by the vast majority of Frenchmen. Henry III., as she well knew, did not intend or desire to exterminate the Huguenots. If that turbulent faction had been openly abetted in its arrogant claims by English assistance, he would have been obliged to become the mere instrument of Elizabeth's worst enemies, Guise and the Holy League. France would have ceased to be any counterpoise to Spain. The English Queen had so skilfully played a most difficult and delicate game that Henry of Navarre had been able to keep his head above water; Guise had upon the whole been held in check; the royal authority, though impaired, had still controlled the foreign policy of France, and so, since 1572, had given England a firm and useful ally. As long as this balanced situation could be maintained, England was safe.

But the time was now at hand when this nice equilibrium of forces would be disturbed by events which neither Elizabeth nor any one else could help. Alençon, the last of the Valois line, was dying. When he should be gone, the next heir to the French King would be no other than the Huguenot Henry of Bourbon, King of the tiny morsel of Navarre that lay north of the Pyrenees. Henry III. wished to recognise his right. But it was impossible that Guise or Philip, or the French nation itself, should tolerate this prospect. Thus the great war of religion which Elizabeth had so carefully abstained from stirring up was now inevitable. The French alliance, the key-stone of her policy, was about to crumble away with the authority of the French King which she had buttressed up. He would be compelled either to become the mere instrument of the Papal party or to combine openly with the Huguenot leader. In either case, Guise, not Henry III., would be the virtual sovereign, and Elizabeth's alliance would not be with France but with a French faction. She would thus be forced into the position which she had hitherto refused to accept—that of sole protector of French and Dutch Protestants, and open antagonist of Spain. The more showy part she was now to play has been the chief foundation of her glory with posterity. It is a glory which she deserves. The most industrious disparagement will never rob her of it. But the sober student will be of opinion that her reputation as a statesman has a more solid basis in the skill and firmness with which during so many years she staved off the necessity for decisive action.

Although the discovery of the Throgmorton plot (Nov. 1583), and the consequent expulsion of the Spanish ambassador, Mendoza, were not immediately followed by open war between England and Spain, yet the course of events thenceforward tended directly to that issue. Elizabeth immediately proposed to the Dutch States to form a naval alliance against Spain, and to concert other measures for mutual defence.

Orange met the offer with alacrity, and pressed Elizabeth to accept the sovereignty of Holland, Zealand, and Utrecht. Perhaps there was no former ruler of England who would not have clutched at such an opportunity of territorial aggrandisement. For Elizabeth it had no charms. Every sensible person now will applaud the sobriety of her aims. But though she eschewed territory, she desired to have military occupation of one or more coast fortresses, at all events for a time, both as a security for the fidelity of the Dutch to any engagements they might make with her, and to enable her to treat on more equal terms with France or Spain, if the Netherlands were destined, after all, to fall into the hands of one of those powers.

While these negotiations were in progress, William of Orange was murdered ($\frac{\text{June 30}}{\text{July 10}}$, 1584). Alençon had died a month earlier. The sovereignty of the revolted Netherlands was thus vacant. Elizabeth advised a joint protectorate by France and England. But the Dutch had small confidence in protectorates, especially of the joint kind. What they wanted was a sovereign, and as Elizabeth would not accept them as her subjects they offered themselves to Henry III. But after nibbling at the offer for eight months Henry was obliged to refuse it. His openly expressed intention to recognise the King of Navarre as his heir had caused a revival of the Holy League. During the winter 1584-5 its reorganisation was busily going on. Philip promised to subsidise it. Mendoza, now ambassador at Paris, was its life and soul. The insurrection was on the point of breaking out. Henry III.

knew that the vast majority of Frenchmen were Catholics. To accept the Dutch offer would, he feared, drive them all into the ranks of the Holy League. He therefore dismissed the Dutch envoys with the recommendation that they should apply to England for protection ($\frac{\text{February 28}}{\text{March 10}}$, 1585).

The manifesto of the Leaguers appeared at the end of March (1585). Henry of Navarre was declared incapable, as a Protestant, of succeeding to the crown. Henry III. was summoned to extirpate heresy. To enforce these demands the Leaguers flew to arms all over France. Had Henry III. been a man of spirit he would have placed himself at the head of the loyal Catholics and fought it out. But by the compact of Nemours he conceded all the demands of the League ($\frac{\text{June 28}}{\text{July 7}}$, 1585). Thus began the last great war of religion, which lasted till Henry of Navarre was firmly seated on the throne of France.

Elizabeth had now finally lost the French alliance, the sheet-anchor of her policy since 1572, and she prepared for the grand struggle which could no longer be averted. As France failed her, she must make the best of the Dutch alliance. She did not conceal from herself that she would have to do her share of the fighting. But she was determined that the Dutch should also do theirs. Deprived of all hope of help from France they wished for annexation to the English crown, because solidarity between the two countries would give them an unlimited claim upon English resources. Elizabeth uniformly told them, first and last, that nothing should induce her to accept that proposal. She would give them a definite amount of assistance in men and money. But every farthing would have to be repaid when the war was over; and in the meantime she must have Flushing and Brill as security. They must also bind themselves to make proper exertions in their own defence. Gilpin, her agent in Zealand, had warned her that if she showed herself too forward they would simply throw the whole burden of the war upon her. Splendid as had often been the resistance of separate towns when besieged, there had been, from the first, lamentable selfishness and apathy as to measures for combined defence. The States had less than 6000 men in the field—half of them English volunteers—at the very time when they were assuring Elizabeth that, if she would come to their assistance, they could and would furnish 15,000. She was justified in regarding their fine promises with much distrust.

While this discussion was going on, Antwerp was lost. The blame of the delay, if blame there was, must be divided equally between the bargainers. The truth is that, cavil as they might about details, the strength of the English contingent was not the real object of concern to either of them. Each was thinking of something else. Though Elizabeth had so peremptorily refused the sovereignty offered by the United Provinces, they were still bent on forcing it upon her. She, on the other hand, had not given up the hope that her more decisive intervention would drive Philip to make the concessions to his revolted subjects which she had so often urged upon him. In her eyes, Philip's sovereignty over them was indefeasible. They were, perhaps, justified in asserting their ancient constitutional rights. But if those were guaranteed, continuance of the rebellion would be criminal. Moreover, she held that elected deputies were but amateur statesmen, and had better leave the *haute politique* to princes to settle. "Princes," she once told a Dutch deputation, "are not to be charged with breach of faith if they sometimes listen to both sides; for they transact business in a princely way and with a princely understanding such as private persons cannot have." Her promise not to make peace behind their backs was not to be interpreted as literally as if it had been made to a brother prince. It merely bound her—so she contended—not to make peace without safeguarding their interests; that is to say, what she considered to be their true interests. Conduct based on such a theory would not be tolerated now, and was not tamely acquiesced in by the Dutch then. But to speak of it as base and treacherous is an abuse of terms.

It would be impossible to follow in detail the peace negotiations which went on between Elizabeth and Parma up to the very sailing of the Armada (1586-8). The terms on which the Queen was prepared to make peace never varied substantially from first to last. We know very well what they were. She claimed for the Protestants of the Netherlands (who were a minority, perhaps, even in the rebel provinces) precisely the same degree of toleration which she allowed to her own Catholics. They were not to be questioned about their religion; but there was to be no public worship or proselytising. The old constitution, as before Alva, was to be restored, which would have involved the departure of the foreign troops. These terms would not have satisfied the States, and if Philip could have been induced to grant them, the States and Elizabeth must have parted company. But, as he would make no concessions, the Anglo-Dutch alliance could, and did, continue. The cautionary towns she was determined never to give up to any one, unless (first) she was repaid her expenses for which they had been mortgaged, and (secondly) the struggle in the Netherlands was brought to an end on terms which she approved. There was, therefore, never any danger of their being surrendered to Philip, and they did, in fact, remain in Elizabeth's hands till her death.

Elizabeth has been severely censured for selecting Leicester to command the English army in the Netherlands. It is certain that he was marked out by public opinion as the fittest person. The Queen's choice was heartily approved by all her ministers, especially by Walsingham, who kept up the most confidential relations with Leicester, and backed him throughout. Custom prescribed that an English army should be commanded, not by a professional soldier, but by a great nobleman. Among the nobility there were a few who had done a little soldiering in a rough way in Scotland or Ireland, but no one who could be called a professional general. The momentous step which Elizabeth was taking would have lost half its significance in the eyes of Europe if any less conspicuous person than Leicester had been appointed. Moreover, it was essential that the nobleman selected should be able and willing to spend largely out of his own resources. By traditional usage, derived from feudal times, peers who were employed on temporary services not only received no salary, but were expected to defray their own expenses, and defray them handsomely. Never did an English nobleman show more public spirit in this respect than Leicester. He raised every penny he could by mortgaging his estates. He not only paid his own personal expenses, but advanced large sums for military purposes, which his mistress never thought of repaying him. If he effected little as a general, it was because he was not provided with the means. Serious mistakes he certainly made, but they were not of a military kind.

Leicester was now fifty-four, bald, white-bearded, and red-faced, but still imposing in figure, carriage, and dress. To Elizabeth he was dear as the friend of her youth, one who, she was persuaded, had loved her for herself when they were both thirty years younger, and was still her most devoted and trustworthy servant. Burghley she liked and trusted, and all the more since he had become a more docile instrument of her policy. Walsingham, a keener intellect and more independent character, she could not but value, though impatient under his penetrating suspicion and almost constant disapproval. Leicester was the intimate friend, the frequent companion of her leisure hours. None of her younger favourites had supplanted him in her regard. By long intimacy he knew the *molles aditus et tempora* when things might be said without offence which were not acceptable at the council-board. The other ministers were glad to use him for this purpose. There can be no question that his appointment to the command in the Netherlands was meant as the most decisive indication that could be given of Elizabeth's determination to face open war with Philip rather than allow him to establish absolute government in that country.

Since the deaths of Alençon and William of Orange, the United Provinces had been without a ruler. The government had been provisionally carried on by the "States," or deputies from each province. Leicester had come with no other title than that of Lieutenant-General of the Queen's troops. But what the States wanted was not so much a military leader as a sovereign ruler. They therefore urged Leicester to accept the powers and title of Governor-General, the office which had been held by the representatives of Philip. From this it would follow, both logically and practically, that Elizabeth herself stood in the place of Philip—in other words, that she was committed to the sovereignty which she had so peremptorily refused.

The offer was accepted by Leicester almost immediately after his arrival (Jan. $\frac{14}{24}$, 1586). There can be little doubt that it was a preconcerted plan between the States and Elizabeth's ministers, who had all along supported the Dutch proposals. Leicester, we know, had contemplated it before leaving England. Davison, who was in Holland, hurried it on, and undertook to carry the news to Elizabeth. Burghley and Walsingham maintained that the step had been absolutely necessary, and implored her not to undo it. Elizabeth herself had suspected that something of the sort would be attempted, and had strictly enjoined

Leicester at his departure to accept no such title. It was not that she wished his powers—that is to say, her own powers—to be circumscribed. On the contrary, she desired that they should in practice be as large and absolute as possible. What she objected to was the title, with all the consequences it involved. And what enraged her most of all was the attempt of her servants to push the thing through behind her back, on the calculation that she would be obliged to accept the accomplished fact. Her wrath vented itself on all concerned, on her ministers, on the States, and on Leicester. To the latter she addressed a characteristic letter:—

"*To my Lord of Leicester from the Queen by Sir Thomas Heneage.* .

"How contemptuously we conceive ourself to have been used by you, you shall by this bearer understand, whom we have expressly sent unto you to charge you withal. We could never have imagined, had we not seen it fall out in experience, that a man raised up by ourself and extraordinarily favoured by us above any other subject of this land, would have in so contemptible [contemptuous] a sort, broken our commandment, in a cause that so greatly toucheth us in honour; whereof although you have showed yourself to make but little account, in most undutiful a sort, you may not therefore think that we have so little care of the reparation thereof as we mind to pass so great a wrong in silence unredressed. And therefore our express pleasure and command is that, all delays and excuses laid apart, you do presently, on the duty of your allegiance, obey and fulfil whatsoever the bearer hereof shall direct you to do in our name. Whereof fail not, as you will answer the contrary at your uttermost peril."

Nor were these cutting reproaches reserved for his private perusal. She severely rebuked the States for encouraging "a creature of her own" to disobey her injunctions, and, as a reparation from them and from him, she required that he should make a public resignation of the government in the place where he had accepted it.

It is not to be wondered at that Elizabeth should think the vindication of her outraged authority to be the most pressing requirement of the moment. But the result was unfortunate for the object of the expedition. The States had conferred "absolute" authority upon Leicester, and would have thought it a cheap price to pay if, by their adroit manœuvre, they had succeeded in forcing the Queen's hand. But they did not care to intrust absolute powers to a mere general of an English contingent. After long discussion, Elizabeth was at length persuaded that the least of evils was to allow him to retain the title which the States had conferred on him (June 1586). But in the meantime they had repented of their haste in letting power go out of their own hands. Their efforts were thenceforth directed to explain away the term "absolute." The long displeasure of the Queen had destroyed the principal value of Leicester in their eyes. He himself had soon incurred their dislike. Impetuous and domineering, he could not endure opposition. Every man who did not fall in with his plans was a malicious enemy, a traitor, a tool of Parma, who ought to be hanged. He still enjoyed the favour of the democratic and bigoted Calvinist party, especially in Utrecht, and he tried to play them off against the States, thereby promoting the rise of the factions which long afterwards distracted the United Provinces. The displeasure of the Queen had taken the shape of not sending him money, and his troops were in great distress and unable to move. Moreover, rumours of the secret peace negotiations were craftily spread by Parma, who, knowing well that they would come to nothing, turned them to the best account by leading the States to suspect that they were being betrayed to Spain.

Elizabeth had sent her army abroad more as a warning to Philip than with a view to active operations. It was no part of her plan to recover any of the territory already conquered by Parma, even if it had lain in her power. She knew that the majority of its inhabitants were Catholics and royalists. She knew also that Parma's attenuated army was considerably outnumbered by the Anglo-Dutch forces, and that he was in dire distress for food and money. The recovered provinces were completely ruined by the war. Their commerce was swept from the sea. The mouths of their great rivers were blockaded. The Protestants of Flanders and Brabant had largely migrated to the unsubdued provinces, whose prosperity, notwithstanding the burdens of war, was advancing by leaps and bounds. Their population was about two millions. That of England itself was little more than four. Religion was no longer the only or the chief motive of their resistance. For even the Catholics among them, who were still very numerous—some said a majority —keenly relished the material prosperity which had grown with independence. Encouraged by English protection, the States were in no humour to listen to compromise. But a compromise was what Elizabeth desired. She was therefore not unwilling that her forces should be confined to an attitude of observation, till it should appear whether her open intervention would extract from Philip such concessions as she deemed reasonable.

Leicester was eager to get to work, and he was warmly supported by Walsingham. Burghley's conduct was less straightforward. He had long found it advisable to cultivate amicable relations with the favourite. He had probably concurred in the plan for making him Governor-General. Even now he was professing to take his part. In reality he was not sorry to see him under a cloud; and though he sympathised as much as ever with the Dutch, he cared more for crippling his rival. Hence his activity in those obscure peace negotiations which he so carefully concealed from Leicester and Walsingham. To keep Walsingham long in the dark, on that or any other subject, was indeed impossible. It was found necessary at last to let him be present at an interview with the agents employed by Burghley and Parma, which brought their backstairs diplomacy to an abrupt conclusion. "They that have been the employers of them," he wrote to Leicester, "are ashamed of the matter." The negotiations went on through other channels, but never made any serious progress.

To compel Philip to listen to a compromise, without at the same time emboldening the Dutch to turn a deaf ear to it—such was the problem which Elizabeth had set herself. She therefore preferred to apply pressure in other quarters. Towards the end of 1585, Drake appeared on the coast of Spain itself, and plundered Vigo. Then crossing the Atlantic, he sacked and burned St. Domingo and Carthagena. Again in 1587, he forced his way into Cadiz harbour, burnt all the shipping and the stores collected for the Armada, and for two months plundered and destroyed every vessel he met off the coast of Portugal.

Philip had so long and so tamely submitted to the many injuries and indignities which Elizabeth heaped upon him, that it is not wonderful if she had come to think that he would never pluck up courage to retaliate. This time she was wrong. The conquest of England had always had its place in his overloaded programme. But it was to be in that hazy ever-receding future, when he should have put down the Dutch rebellion and neutralised France. Elizabeth's open intervention in the Netherlands at length induced him to change his plan. England, he now decided, must be first dealt with.

In the meantime, Parma's operations in the Netherlands were starved quite as much as Leicester's. Plundering excursions, two or three petty combats not deserving the name of battles, half-a-dozen small towns captured on one side or the other—such is the military record from the date of Elizabeth's intervention to the arrival of the Armada. Parma had somewhat the best of this work, such as it was. But the war in the Netherlands was practically stagnant.

At the end of the first year of Leicester's government, events of the highest importance obliged him to pay a visit to England (Nov. 1586). The Queen of Scots had been found guilty of conspiring to assassinate Elizabeth, and Parliament had been summoned to decide upon her fate.

CHAPTER IX

EXECUTION OF THE QUEEN OF SCOTS: 1584-1587

THROGMORTON's plot—of which the Queen of Scots was undoubtedly cognisant, though it was not pressed against her—brought home to every one the danger in which Elizabeth stood (1584). To the Catholic conspiracy, the temptation to take her life was enormous. It was becoming clear that, while she lived, the much talked of insurrection would never come off. The large majority of Catholics would have nothing to do with it —still less with foreign invasion. They would obey their lawful sovereign. But if once Elizabeth were dead, by whatever means, their lawful sovereign would be Mary. The rebels would be the Protestants, if they should try to place any one else on the throne. The Protestants had no organisation. They had no candidate for the crown ready. It was to be feared that no great noble would step forward to lead them. Burghley himself, though longing as much as ever for Mary's head, had with a prudent eye to all eventualities, contrived some time before to persuade her that he was her well-wisher. Houses of Commons, it is true, had shown themselves strongly and increasingly Protestant. But with the demise of the crown, Parliament, if in being at the time, would be *ipso facto* dissolved. The Privy Council, in like manner, would cease to have any legal existence. Burghley, Walsingham, and the other new men of whom it was mostly composed, had no power or weight, except as instruments of the sovereign. Her death would leave them helpless. The country would take its direction not from them, but from the great nobles of large ancestral possessions. Nor could they provide for such an emergency by privately selecting a Protestant successor beforehand, and privately organising their partisans. It would have been as much as their lives were worth if their mistress had caught them doing anything of the kind.

In this dilemma an ingenious plan suggested itself to them. They drew up a "Bond of Association," by which the subscribers engaged that, if the Queen were murdered, they would never accept as successor any one " by whom *or for whom* " such act should be committed, but would " prosecute such person to death."

This was a hypothetical way of excluding Mary and organising a Protestant resistance to which Elizabeth could make no objection. But the ministers knew that, as a merely voluntary association without Parliamentary sanction, it would add little strength or confidence to the Protestant party. It would not even test their numbers; for no Marian ventured to refuse the oath. Mary herself desired to be allowed to take it. The bond was therefore converted into a Statute by Parliament, though not without some important alterations (March 1585). It was enacted that if the realm was invaded, or a rebellion instigated, by *or for* any one pretending a title to the succession, or if the Queen's murder was plotted by any one, or with the privity of any one that pretended title, such pretender, *after examination and judgment* by an extraordinary commission to be nominated by the Queen, and consisting of at least twenty-four privy councillors and lords of Parliament assisted by the chief judges, should be excluded from the succession, and that, on proclamation of the sentence and direction by the Queen, all subjects might and should pursue the offender to death. If the Queen were murdered, the lords of the Council at the time of her death, or the majority of them, should join to themselves at least twelve other lords of Parliament not making title to the crown, and the chief judges; and if, after examination, they should come to the above-mentioned conclusion, they should without delay, by all forcible and possible means, prosecute the guilty persons to death, and should have power to raise and use such forces as should in that behalf be needful and convenient; and no subjects should be liable to punishment for anything done according to the tenor of the Statute.

Here, then, was a legal way provided by which the Protestant ministers might act against Mary if Elizabeth were murdered. They were in fact created a Provisional Government, with power to exclude Mary from the throne. Whether they would have the courage or strength to do so remained to be seen; but they would at least have formal law on their side.

It had never entered into Mary's plans to wait for Elizabeth's natural death. She therefore read the new Act as a sentence of exclusion. Another blow soon fell on her. In 1584, elated by her son's victory over the raiders of Ruthven, and believing that he was willing to recognise her joint sovereignty and cooperate with a Guise invasion, she had scornfully refused the last overtures that Elizabeth ever made to her. She now learnt that he had never intended to accept association with her, and that he had urged Elizabeth not to release her. In the following year he had accepted an annual pension of £4000 with some grumbling at its amount; and a defensive alliance was at length concluded between the two countries, Mary's name not being mentioned in the treaty (July 1586).

As the prospects of the Scottish Queen became darker both in England and her own country, she grew more desperate and reckless. Early in 1586, Walsingham contrived a way of regularly inspecting all her most secret correspondence. He soon discovered that she was encouraging Babington's plot for assassinating Elizabeth. Some of the conspirators, though avowed Catholics, had offices in the royal household; such was Elizabeth's easy-going confidence. It was hoped that Parma would at the moment of the murder land troops on the east coast. Mendoza, now Spanish ambassador in Paris, warmly encouraged the project.

The Scottish Queen was now in the case contemplated by the Statute of the previous year. But it required all the urgency of the Council to prevail with Elizabeth to have her brought to trial. Elizabeth's whole conduct shows that she would even now have preferred to deal with her rival as she did in the inquiry into the Darnley murder. She would have been content to discredit her, to expose her guilt, and, if possible, to bring her to her knees confessing her crimes and pleading for mercy. But Mary was not of the temper to confess. Humiliation and effacement were to her worse than death. She chose to brazen it out with a well-grounded confidence that, as long as she asserted her innocence, people would always be found to believe in it, let the evidence be what it would. Besides, long impunity had convinced her that Elizabeth did not dare to take her life.

There was nothing for it, therefore, but to bring her to trial. A Special Commission was nominated under the provisions of the Statute of 1585, consisting of forty-five persons—peers, privy councillors, and judges—who proceeded to Fotheringay Castle, whither Mary had been removed.[1] She at first refused their jurisdiction; but on being informed that they would proceed in her absence, she appeared before them under protest (October 14, 1586). After sitting at Fotheringay for two days, the Court adjourned to Westminster, where it pronounced her guilty (October 25).[2] A declaration was added that her disqualification for the succession, which followed by the Statute, did not affect any rights that her son might possess. The verdict was immediately known; but its proclamation was deferred till Parliament could be consulted.

[1] Some persons whose names do not appear in the Commission sat on the trial, while some who were appointed did not sit.
[2] Those who wish to know the grounds on which Mary's complicity in Babington's plot has been denied can consult Lingard, Tytler, and Labanoff. In my opinion, their arguments are very feeble.

A general election had been held while the trial was going on, and Parliament met four days after its conclusion (October 20). The whole evidence was gone into afresh. Not a word seems to have been said in Mary's favour; and an address was presented to the Queen praying for execution. If precedents were wanted for the capital punishment of an anointed sovereign, there were the cases of Agag, Jezebel, Athaliah, Deiotarus, king of Galatia, put to death by Julius Cæsar, Rhescuporis, king of Thrace, by Tiberius, and Conradin by Charles of Anjou. In vain did Elizabeth request them to reconsider their vote, and devise some other expedient. Usually so deferential to her suggestions, they reiterated their declaration that "the Queen's safety could no way be secured as long as the Queen of Scots lived."

Elizabeth's hesitation has been generally set down to hypocrisy. It has been taken for granted that she desired Mary's death, and was glad to have it pressed upon her by her subjects. I believe that her reluctance was most genuine. If not of generous disposition, neither was she revengeful or cruel. She had no animosity against her enemies. She lacked gall. She was never in any hurry to punish the disaffected, or even to weed them out of her service. She rather prided herself on employing them even about her person. Since her accession only two English peers had been put to death, though several had richly deserved it. She could affirm with perfect truth that, for the last fifteen years, she, and she alone, had stood between Mary and the scaffold, and this at great and increasing risk to her own life.

There had, perhaps, been a time when to destroy the prospect of a Catholic succession would have driven the Catholics into rebellion. But that time had long gone by, as every one knew. Elizabeth had only two dangers now to fear, invasion and assassination, the latter being the most threatening. There would be little inducement to attempt it if Mary were not alive to profit by it. Yet Elizabeth hesitated. The explanation of her reluctance is very simple. She flinched from the obloquy, the undeserved obloquy, which she saw was in store for her. Careless to an extraordinary degree about her personal danger, she would have preferred, as far as she was herself concerned, to let Mary live. It was her ministers and the Protestant party who, for their own interest, were forcing her to shed her cousin's blood; and it seemed to her unfair that the undivided odium should fall, as she foresaw it would fall, on her alone.

The suspense continued through December and January. In the meantime it became abundantly clear that no foreign court would interfere actively to save Mary's life. While she had been growing old in captivity, new interests had sprung up, fresh schemes had been formed in which she had no place. She stood in the way of half-a-dozen ambitions. Everybody was weary of her and her wrongs and her pretensions. The Pope had felt less interest of late in a princess whose rights, if established, would pass to a Protestant heir. Philip could not intercede for her even if he had desired to save her life. He was already at war with England, and, if she had known it, not with any intention of supporting her claims.[1] James by his recent treaty with England had tacitly treated his mother as an enemy. Her scheme for kidnapping and disinheriting him, found among her papers at Chartley, had been promptly communicated to him. Decency required that he should make a show of remonstrance and menace. But he had every reason to desire her death, and his only thought was to use the opportunity for extorting from Elizabeth a recognition of his title to the English crown and an increase of his pension. He sent the Master of Gray to drive this bargain. The very choice of his envoy, the man who had persuaded him to break with his mother, showed Elizabeth how the land lay, and she did not think it worth her while to bribe him in either way. The Marian nobles blustered and called for war. Not one of them wanted to see Mary back in Scotland or cared what became of her; but they had got an idea that Philip would pay them for a plundering raid into England, and the doubly lucrative prospect was irresistible. James, however, though pretending resentment and really sulky at his rebuff, knew his own interests too well to quarrel with England. What the action of the French King was is less certain. Openly he remonstrated with considerable vigour and persistence; not entering into the question of Mary's guilt, but protesting against the punishment of a Queen and a member of his family. Probably his efforts, so far as they went, were sincere, for he instructed his ambassador to bribe the English ministers if possible to save her life. But it was evident that, however offended Henry III. might be

[1] There was no formal proclamation of war on either side.

by the execution of his sister-in-law, he would not be provoked into playing the game of Spain.

A warrant for the execution had been drawn soon after the adjournment of Parliament, and all through December and January Elizabeth's ministers kept urging her to sign it. At length, when the Scotch and French ambassadors were gone, and with them the last excuse for delay, she signed it in the presence of Davison (who had lately been made co-secretary with Walsingham), and directed him to have it sealed (February 1). What else passed between them on that occasion must always remain uncertain, because Davison's four written statements, and his answers at his trial, differ in important particulars not only from the Queen's account but from one another. So much, however, will to most persons who examine the evidence be very clear. Elizabeth meant the execution to take place. There is no reason to doubt Davison's statement that she "forbade him to trouble her any further, or let her hear any more thereof till it was done, seeing that for her part she had now performed all that either in law or reason could be required of her." But signing the warrant, as both of them knew, was not enough. The formal delivery of it to some person, with direction to carry it out, was the final step necessary. This, by Davison's own admission, the Queen managed to evade. He saw that she wished to thrust the responsibility upon him and Walsingham, and he suspected that she meant to disavow them. Although, therefore, she had enjoined strict secrecy, he laid the matter before Hatton and Burghley.

Burghley assembled in his own room the Earls of

Derby and Leicester, Lords Howard of Effingham, Hunsdon, and Cobham, Knollys, Hatton, Walsingham, and Davison (February 3). These ten were probably the only privy councillors then at Greenwich.[1] He laid before them Davison's statement of what had passed between the Queen and himself at both interviews. He said that she had done as much as could be expected of her; that she evidently wished her ministers to take whatever responsibility remained upon themselves without informing her; and that they ought to do so. His proposal was agreed to. A letter was written to the Earls of Kent and Shrewsbury instructing them to carry out the execution. This letter all the ten signed, and it was at once despatched along with the warrant. They quite understood that Elizabeth would disavow them. They saw that she wished to have a pretext for saying that Mary had been put to death without her knowledge, and before she had finally made up her mind. They were willing to furnish her with this pretext. Of course there would be more or less of a storm to keep up the make-believe. But ten privy councillors acting together could not well be punished.

On Thursday (February 9) the news of the execution arrived. Elizabeth now learnt for the first time that the responsibility which she had intended to fix on the two secretaries, one a nobody and the other no favourite, had been shared by eight others of the Council, includ-

[1] The remaining Privy Councillors were Archbishop Whitgift, Lord Chancellor Bromley, the Earls of Shrewsbury and Warwick, Lord Buckhurst, Sir James Crofts, Sir Ralph Sadler, Sir Walter Mildmay, Sir Amyas Paulet, and the Latin Secretary, Wolley.

ing all its most important members. Storm at them the might and did, and all the more furiously because they had combined for self-protection. But to punish she whole ten was out of the question. Yet if no one were punished, with what face could she tender her improbable explanation to foreign courts? The unlucky Davison was singled out. He could be charged with divulging what he had been ordered to keep secret and misleading the others. He was tried before a Special Commission, fined 10,000 marks, and imprisoned for some time in the Tower. The fine was rigidly exacted, and it reduced him to poverty. Burghley, whose tool he had been almost as much as Elizabeth's, took pains to make his disgrace permanent, because he wanted the secretaryship for his son, Robert Cecil.

The strange thing is, that Elizabeth not only expected her transparent falsehoods to be formally accepted as satisfactory, but hoped that they would be really believed. Her letter to James was an insult to his understanding. "I would you knew (though not felt) the extreme dolour that overwhelms my mind, for that miserable accident which (far contrary to my meaning) hath befallen. . . . I beseech you that as God and many more know how innocent I am in this case, so you will believe me that if I had bid [bidden] ought I would have bid [abided] by it. . . . Thus assuring yourself of me that as I know this [the execution] was deserved, yet if I had meant it I would never lay it on others' shoulders, no more will I not damnify myself that thought it not."

Little as James cared what became of his mother,

it was impossible that he should not feel humiliated when he was expected to swallow such a pill as this —and ungilded too. He had no intention of going to war with the country of which he might now at any moment become the legitimate King. But to let Elizabeth see that unless he was paid he could be disagreeable, he winked at raids across the border and coquetted with the faction who were inviting Philip to send a Spanish army to Scotland. It was but a passing display of temper. The end of the year (1587) saw him again drawing close to Elizabeth, and she was able to give her undivided attention to the coming Armada.

It cannot be seriously maintained that because Mary was not an English subject she could not be lawfully tried and punished for crimes committed in England. Those, if any there now be, who adopt her own contention that, being an anointed Queen, she was not amenable to any earthly tribunal, but to God alone, are beyond the reach of earthly argument. The English government had a right to detain her as a dangerous public enemy. She, on the other hand, had a right to resist such restraint if she could, and she might have carried conspiracy very far without incurring our blame. But for good reasons we draw a line at conspiracy to murder. No government ever did or will let it pass unpunished. If Napoleon at St. Helena had engaged in conspiracies for seizing the island, no one could have blamed him, even though they might have involved bloodshed. But if he had been convicted of plotting the assassination of Sir Hudson Lowe, he would assuredly have been hanged.

That the execution was a wise and opportune stroke of policy can hardly be disputed. It broke up the Catholic party in England at the moment when their disaffection was about to be tempted by the appearance of the Armada. There had been a time when they had hopes of James. But he was now known to be a stiff Protestant. Only the small Jesuitical faction was prepared to accept Philip either as an heir of John of Gaunt or as Mary's legatee. There was no other Catholic with a shadow of a claim. The bulk of the party therefore ceased to look forward to a restoration of the old religion, and rallied to the cause of national independence.

NOTE ON PAULET'S ALLEGED REFUSAL TO MURDER MARY.

I have not alluded in the text to the story, generally repeated by historians, that Elizabeth urged Paulet and Drury to murder Mary privately. There is no doubt that, after the signature of the warrant, Walsingham and Davison, by Elizabeth's direction, urged Paulet and Drury to put Mary to death, and that they refused. But was it a private murder that was meant or a public execution without delivery of the warrant? There is nothing in any of Davison's statements inconsistent with the latter and far more probable explanation. The blacker charge is founded solely on the two letters which are generally accepted as being those which passed between the secretaries and Paulet, but which may be confidently set down as impudent forgeries. They were first given to the world in 1722 by Dr. George Mackenzie, a violent Marian, who says that *a copy* of them was sent him by Mr. Urry of Christ Church, Oxford, and that they had been found among Paulet's papers. Two years later they were printed by Hearne, an Oxford Jacobite and Nonjuror, who says he got them from *a copy* furnished him by a friend unnamed (Urry?), who told him he had *copied* them in 1717 from a MS. letter-book of

Paulet's. There is also a MS. *copy* in the Harleian collection, which contains erasures and emendations—an extraordinary thing in a copy. It is said to be in the handwriting of the Earl of Oxford himself. There is nothing to show whence he copied it.

No one has ever seen the originals of these letters. Neither has any one, except Hearne's unnamed friend, seen the "letter-book" into which Paulet is supposed to have copied them. Where had this "letter-book" been before 1717? Where was it in 1717? What became of it after 1717? To none of these questions is there any answer. The most rational conclusion is that the "letter-book" never existed, and that the letters were fabricated in the reign of George I. by some Oxford Jacobite, who thought it easier and more prudent to circulate *copies* than to attempt an imitation of Paulet's well-known handwriting, with all the other difficulties involved in forging a manuscript.

But it may be said, Do not the letters fit in with Davison's narrative? Of course they do. It was for the very purpose of putting an odious meaning on that narrative that they were fabricated. It was known that letters about putting Mary to death had passed. The real letters had never been seen, and had doubtless been destroyed. Here therefore was a fine opportunity for manufacturing spurious ones.

CHAPTER X

WAR WITH SPAIN : 1587-1603

ELIZABETH is not seen at her best in war. She did not easily resign herself to its sacrifices. It frightened her to see the money which she had painfully put together, pound by pound, during so many years, by many a small economy, draining out at the rate of £17,000 a month into the bottomless pit of military expenditure. When Leicester came back she simply stopped all remittances to the Netherlands, making sure that if she did not feed her soldiers some one else would have to do it. She saw that Parma was not pressing forward. And though rumours of the enormous preparations in Spain, which accounted for his inactivity, continued to pour in, she still hoped that her intervention in the Netherlands was bending Philip to concessions. All this time Parma was steadily carrying out his master's plans for the invasion. His little army was to be trebled in the autumn by reinforcements principally from Italy. In the meantime he was collecting a flotilla of flat-bottomed boats. As soon as the Armada should appear they were to make the passage under its protection.

It would answer no useful purpose, even if my limits permitted it, to enter into the particulars of Elizabeth's policy towards the United Provinces during the twelve months that preceded the appearance of the Armada. Her proceedings were often tortuous, and by setting them forth in minute detail her detractors have not found it difficult to represent them as treacherous. But, living three centuries later, what have we to consider but the general scope and drift of her policy? Looking at it as a whole we shall find that, whether we approve of it or not, it was simple, consistent, and undisguised. She had no intention of abandoning the Provinces to Philip, still less of betraying them. But she did wish them to return to their allegiance, if she could procure for them proper guarantees for such liberties as they had been satisfied with before Philip's tyranny began. If Philip had been wise he would have made those concessions. Elizabeth is not to be over-much blamed if she clung too long to the belief that he could be persuaded or compelled to do what was so much for his own interest. If she was deceived so was Burghley. Walsingham is entitled to the credit of having from first to last refused to believe that the negotiations were anything but a blind.

Though Elizabeth desired peace, she did not cease to deal blows at Philip. In the spring of 1587 (April-June), while she was most earnestly pushing her negotiations with Parma, she despatched Drake on a new expedition to the Spanish coast. He forced his way into the harbours of Cadiz and Corunna, destroyed many ships and immense stores, and came back loaded with plunder. The Armada had not been crippled, for most of the ships that were to compose it were lying in the Tagus. But the concentration had been delayed. Fresh stores had to be collected. Drake calculated, and as it proved rightly, that another season at least would be consumed in repairing the loss, and that England, for that summer and autumn, could rest secure of invasion.

The delay was most unwelcome to Philip. The expense of keeping such a fleet and army on foot through the winter would be enormous. Spain was maintaining not only the Armada but the army of Parma; for the resources of the Netherlands, which had been the true El Dorado of the Spanish monarchy, were completely dried up. So impatient was Philip —usually the slowest of men—that he proposed to despatch the Armada even in September, and actually wrote to Parma that he might expect it at any moment. But, as Drake had calculated, September was gone before everything was ready. The naval experts protested against the rashness of facing the autumnal gales, with no friendly harbour on either side of the Channel in which to take refuge. Philip then made the absurd suggestion that the army from the Netherlands should cross by itself in its flat-bottomed boats. But Parma told him that it was absolutely out of the question. Four English ships could sink the whole flotilla. In the meantime his soldiers, waiting on the Dunkirk Downs and exposed to the severities of the weather, were dying off like flies. Philip and Elizabeth resembled one another in this, that neither of them had any personal experience of war either by land or sea. For a Queen this was natural. For a King it was unnatural, and for an ambitious King unprecedented. They did not understand the proper adaptation of means to ends. Yet it was necessary to obtain their sanction before anything could be done. Hence there was much mismanagement on both sides. Still England was in no real danger during the summer and autumn of 1587, because Philip's preparations were not completed; and before the end of the year the English fleet was lying in the Channel. But the Queen grudged the expense of keeping the crews up to their full complement. The supply of provisions and ammunition was also very inadequate. The expensiveness of war is generally a sufficient reason for not going to war; but to attempt to do war cheaply is always unwise. "Sparing and war," as Effingham observed, " have no affinity together."

Drake strongly urged that, instead of trying to guard the Channel, the English fleet should make for the coast of Spain, and boldly assail the Armada as soon as it put to sea. This was the advice of a man who had all the shining qualities of Nelson, and seems to have been in no respect his inferior. It was no counsel of desperation. He was confident of success. Lord Howard of Effingham, the Admiral, was of the same opinion. The negotiations were odious to him. For Burghley, who clings to them, he has no more reverence than Hamlet had for Polonius. "Since England was England," he writes to Walsingham, "there was never such a stratagem and mask to deceive her as this treaty of peace. I pray God that we do not curse for this a long grey beard with a white head witless, that will make all the world think us heartless. You know whom I mean."

With the hopes and fears of these sea-heroes, it is

instructive to compare the forecast of the great soldier who was to conduct the invasion. Always obedient and devoted to his sovereign, Parma played his part in the deceptive negotiations with consummate skill. But his own opinion was that it would be wise to negotiate in good faith and accept the English terms. Though prepared to undertake the invasion, he took a very serious view of the risks to be encountered. He tells Philip that the English preparations are formidable both by land and sea. Even if the passage should be safely accomplished, disembarkation would be difficult. His army, reduced by the hardships of the winter from 30,000 men, which he had estimated as the proper number, to less than 17,000, was dangerously small for the work expected of it. He would have to fight battle after battle, and the further he advanced the weaker would his army become both from losses and from the necessity of protecting his communications.

Parma had carefully informed himself of the preparations in England. From the beginning of Elizabeth's reign, attention had been paid to the organisation, training, and equipment of the militia, and especially since the relations with Spain had become more hostile. On paper it seems to have amounted to 117,000 men. Mobilisation was a local business. Sir John Norris drew up the plan of defence. Beacon fires did the work of the telegraph. Every man knew whither he was to repair when their blaze should be seen. The districts to be abandoned, the positions to be defended, the bridges to be broken, were all marked out. Three armies, calculated to amount in the aggregate to 73,000 men, were ordered to assemble in July. Whether so many were actually mustered is doubtful. But Parma would certainly have found himself confronted by forces vastly superior in numbers to his own, and would have had, as he said, to fight battle after battle. The bow had not been entirely abandoned, but the greater part of the archers—two-thirds in some counties—had lately been armed with calivers. What was wanting in discipline would have been to some extent made up by the spontaneous cohesion of a force organised under its natural leaders, the nobles and gentry of each locality, not a few of whom had seen service abroad. But, after all, the greatest element of strength was the free spirit of the people. England was, and had long been, a nation of freemen. There were a few peers, and a great many knights and gentlemen. But there was no noble caste, as on the Continent, separated by an impassable barrier of birth and privilege from the mass of the people. All felt themselves fellow-countrymen bound together by common sentiments, common interests, and mutual respect.

This spirit of freedom—one might almost say of equality—made itself felt still more in the navy, and goes far to account for the cheerful energy and dash with which every service was performed. "The English officers lived on terms of sympathy with their men unknown to the Spaniards, who raised between the commander and the commanded absurd barriers of rank and blood which forbade to his pride any labour but that of fighting. Drake touched the true mainspring of English success when he once (in his voyage round the world) indignantly rebuked some coxcomb gentlemen-adventurers with, 'I should like to see the gentleman that will refuse to set his hand to a rope. I must have the gentlemen to hale and draw with the mariners.'"[1] Drake, Hawkins, Frobisher were all born of humble parents. They rose by their own valour and capacity. They had gentlemen of birth serving under them. To Howard and Cumberland and Seymour they were brothers-in-arms. The master of every little trading vessel was fired by their example, and hoped to climb as high.

It is the pleasure of some writers to speak of Elizabeth's naval preparations as disgracefully insufficient, and to treat the triumphant result as a sort of miracle. To their apprehension, indeed, her whole reign is one long interference by Providence with the ordinary relations of cause and effect. The number of royal ships as compared with those of private owners in the fleet which met the great Armada— 34 to 161—is represented as discreditably small. By Englishmen of that day, it was considered to be creditably large. Sir Edward Coke (who was thirty-eight at the time of the Armada), writing under Charles I., when the royal navy was much larger, says: "In the reign of Queen Elizabeth (I being then acquainted with this business) there were thirty-three [royal ships] besides pinnaces, which so guarded and regarded the navigation of the merchants, as they had safe vent for their commodities, and trade and traffic flourished."[2]

It seems to be overlooked that the royal navy,

[1] Kingsley, *Westward Ho.* [2] *Institutes,* Fourth Part, Chap. I.

such as it was, was almost the creation of Elizabeth. Her father was the first English king who made any attempt to keep a standing navy of his own. He established the Admiralty and the first royal dockyard. Under Edward and Mary the navy, like everything else, went to ruin. Elizabeth's ship-building, humble as it seems to us, excited the admiration of her subjects, and was regarded as one of the chief advances of her reign. The ships, when not in commission, were kept in the Medway. The Queen personally paid the greatest attention to them. They were always kept in excellent condition, and could be fitted out for sea at very short notice. Economy was enforced in this, as in other departments, but not at the expense of efficiency. The wages of officers and men were very much augmented; but in the short periods for which crews were enlisted, and in the victualling, there seems to have been unwise parsimony in 1588. The grumbling of alarmists about unpreparedness, apathy, stinginess, and red-tape was precisely what it is in our own day. We know that some allowance is to be made for it.

The movements of the Armada were perfectly well known in England, and all the dispositions to meet it at sea were completed in a leisurely manner. Conferences were still going on at Ostend between English and Spanish commissioners. On the part of Elizabeth there was sincerity, but not blind credulity nor any disposition to make unworthy concessions. Conferences quite as protracted have often been held between belligerents while hostilities were being actively carried on. The large majority of Englishmen were resolved to fight to the death against any invader. But, as against Spain, there was not that eager pugnacity which a war with France always called forth, except, perhaps, among the sea-rovers; and even they would have contented themselves, if it had been possible, with the unrecognised privateering which had so long given them the profits of war with the immunities of peace. The rest of the nation respected their Queen for her persevering endeavour to find a way of reconciliation with an ancient ally, and to limit, in the meantime, the area of hostilities. They were confident, and with good reason, that she would surrender no important interest, and that aggressive designs would be met, as they had always been met, more than half-way.

The story of the great victory is too well known to need repetition here. But some comments are necessary. It is usual, for one reason or other, to exaggerate the disparity of the opposing fleets, and to represent England as only saved from impending ruin by the extraordinary daring of her seamen, and a series of fortunate accidents. The final destruction of the Armada, after the pursuit was over, was certainly the work of wind and sea. But if we fairly weigh the available strength on each side, we shall see that the English commanders might from the first feel, as they did feel, a reasonable assurance of defeating the invaders.

Let us first compare the strength of the fleets:

ENGLISH.	Ships.	Tonnage.	Guns.	Mariners.
Royal	34	11850	837	6279
Private	163	17894	not stated	9506
	197	29744		15785
SPANISH.	132	59120	3165	8766

The Armada carried besides 21,855 soldiers.[1] The first thing that strikes us is the immense preponderance in tonnage on the part of the Spaniards, and in sailors on the part of the English. This really goes far to explain the result. Nothing is more certain than that the Spanish ships, notwithstanding their superior size, were for fighting and sailing purposes very inferior to the English. It had always been believed that, to withstand the heavy seas of the Atlantic, a ship should be constructed like a lofty fortress. The English builders were introducing lower and longer hulls and a greater spread of canvas. Their crews, as has always been the case in our navy, were equally handy as sailors and gunners. The Spanish ships were under-manned. The soldiers were not accustomed to work the guns, and were of no use unless it came to boarding, which Howard ordered his captains to avoid. The English guns, if fewer than the Spanish, were heavier and worked by more practised men.[2] Their balls not only cut up the rigging of the Spaniards but tore their hulls (which were supposed to be cannon-proof), while the English ships were hardly touched. The slaughter among the wretched soldiers crowded between decks was terrible. Blood was seen pouring out of the lee-scuppers. "The English ships," says a Spanish officer, "were under such good management that they did with them what they pleased." The work was done almost entirely by the Queen's ships. "If you had

---

[1] These figures are taken from Barrow's Life of Drake.

[2] We hear of thirty-three-pounders and even sixty-pounders in the Queen's ships. Whereas the Spanish admiral, sending to Parma for balls, asks for nothing heavier than ten pounds.

seen," says Sir William Winter, "the simple service done by the merchants and coast ships, you would have said we had been little helped by them, otherwise than that they did make a show."

The principal and final battle was fought off Gravelines ($\frac{\text{July 29}}{\text{Aug. 8}}$). The Armada therefore did arrive at its destination, but only to show that the general plan of the invasion was an impracticable one. The superiority in tonnage and number of guns on the morning of that day, though not what it had been when the fighting began a week before, was still immense, if superiority in those particulars had been of any use. But with this battle the plan of Philip was finally shattered. So far from being in a condition to cover Parma's passage, the Spanish admiral was glad to escape as best he could from the English pursuit.

During the eight days' fight, be it observed, the Armada had experienced no unfavourable weather or other stroke of ill-fortune. The wind had been mostly in the west, and not tempestuous. After the last battle, when the crippled Spanish ships were drifting upon the Dutch shoals, it opportunely shifted, and enabled them to escape into the North Sea.

It would not be easy to find any great naval engagement in which the victors suffered so little. In the last battle, when they came to close quarters, they had about sixty killed. During the first seven days their loss seems to have been almost *nil*. One vessel only—not belonging to the Queen—became entangled among the enemy, and succumbed. Except the master of this vessel not one of the captains was killed from first to last. Many men of rank were serving in the fleet. It is not mentioned that one of them was so much as wounded.

Looking at all these facts, we can surely come to only one conclusion. Philip's plan was hopeless from the first. Barring accidents, the English were bound to win. On no other occasion in our history was our country so well prepared to meet her enemies. Never was her safety from invasion so amply guaranteed. The defeat of the Great Armada was the deserved and crowning triumph of thirty years of good government at home and wise policy abroad; of careful provision for defence and sober abstinence from adventure and aggression.

Of the land preparations it is impossible to speak with equal confidence, as they were never put to the test. If the Spaniards had landed, Leicester's militia would no doubt have experienced a bloody defeat. London might have been taken and plundered. But Parma himself never expected to become master of the country without the aid of a great Catholic rising. This, we may affirm with confidence, would not have taken place on even the smallest scale. Overwhelming forces would soon have gathered round the Spaniards. They would probably have retired to the coast, and there fortified some place from which it would have been difficult to dislodge them as long as they retained the command of the sea.

Such seems to have been the utmost success which, in the most favourable event, could have attended the invasion. A great disaster, no doubt, for England, and one for which Elizabeth would have been judged by history with more severity than justice; for Englishmen have always chosen to risk it, down to our own time.[1] No government which insisted on making adequate provision for the military defence of the country would have been tolerated then, or, to all appearance, would be tolerated now. We have always trusted to our navy. It were to be wished that our naval superiority were as assured now as when we defeated the Armada.

The arrangements for feeding the soldiers and sailors were very defective. A praiseworthy system of control had been introduced to check waste and peculation in time of peace. Of course it did not easily adapt itself to the exigencies of war. Military operations are sure to suffer where a certain, or rather uncertain, amount of waste and peculation is not risked. We have not forgotten the "horrible and heart-rending" sufferings of our army in the Crimea, which, like those of Elizabeth's fleet, had to be relieved by private effort. In the sixteenth century the lot of the soldier and sailor everywhere was want and disease, varied at intervals by plunder and excess. Philip's soldiers and sailors were worse off than Elizabeth's, though he grudged no money for purposes of war.

Those who profess to be scandalised by the appointment of Leicester to the command of the army should point out what fitter choice could have been made. He was the only great nobleman with any military experience; and to suppose that any one

[1] The Earl of Sussex, after inspecting the preparations for defence in Hampshire towards the end of 1587, writes to the Council that he had found nothing ready. The "better sort" said, "We are much charged many ways, and when the enemy comes we will provide for him; but he will not come yet."

but a great nobleman could have been appointed to such a command is to show a profound ignorance of the ideas of the time. He had Sir John Norris, a really able soldier, as his marshal of the camp. After all, no one has alleged that he did not do his duty with energy and intelligence. The story that the Queen thought of making him her "Lieutenant in the government of England and Ireland," but was dissuaded from it by Burghley and Hatton, rests on no authority but that of Camden, who is fond of repeating spiteful gossip about Leicester. No sensible person will believe that she meant to create a sort of Grand Vizier. She may have thought of making him what we should call "Commander-in-Chief." There would be much to say for such a concentration of authority while the kingdom was threatened with invasion. The title of "Lieutenant" was a purely military one, and began to be applied under the Tudors to the commanders of the militia in each county. Leicester's title for the time was "Lieutenant and Captain-General of the Queen's armies and companies." But we find him complaining to Walsingham that the patent of Hunsdon, the commander of the Midland army, gave him independent powers. "I shall have wrong if he absolutely command where my patent doth give me power. You may easily conceive what absurd dealings are likely to fall out if you allow two absolute commanders" (28 July). Camden's story is probably a confused echo of this dispute.

Writers who are loth to admit that the trust, the gratitude, the enthusiastic loyalty which Elizabeth inspired were the first and most important cause of the great victory, have sought to belittle the grandest moment of her life by pointing out that the famous speech at Tilbury was made *after* the battle of Gravelines. But the dispersal of the Armada by the storm of August 5th was not yet known in England. Drake, writing on the 8th and 10th, thinks that it is gone to Denmark to refit, and begs the Queen not to diminish any of her forces. The occasion of the speech on the 10th seems to have been the arrival of a post on that day, while the Queen was at dinner in Leicester's tent, with a false alarm that Parma had embarked all his forces, and might be expected in England immediately.[1]

But the Lieutenant-General had reached the end of his career. Three weeks after the Tilbury review he died of "a continued fever," at the age of fifty-six. He kept Elizabeth's regard to the last, because she believed—and during the latter part of his life, not wrongly—in his fidelity and devotion. There is no sign that she at any time valued his judgment or suffered him to sway her policy, except so far as he was the mouthpiece of abler advisers; nor did she ever allow his enmities, violent as they were, to prejudice her against any of her other servants. His fortune was no doubt much above his deserts, and he has paid the usual penalty. There are few personages in history about whom so much malicious nonsense has been written.

We cannot help looking on England as placed in a quite new position by the defeat of the Armada—a

[1] Sir Edward Radcliffe to the Earl of Sussex.—*Ellis*, 2nd Series, vol. iii. p. 142.

position of security and independence. In truth, what was changed was not so much the relative strength of England and Spain as the opinion of it held by Englishmen and Spaniards, and indeed by all Europe. The loss to Philip in mere ships, men, and treasure was no doubt considerable. But his inability to conquer England was demonstrated rather than caused by the destruction of the Armada. Philip himself talked loftily about "placing another fleet upon the seas." But his subjects began to see that defence, not conquest, was now their business—and had been for some time if they had only known it:

> Cervi, luporum præda rapacium,
> Sectamur ultro quos opimus
> Fallere et effugere est triumphus.

Elizabeth's attitude to Philip underwent a marked change. Till then she had been unwilling to abandon the hope of a peaceful settlement. She had dealt him not a few stinging blows, but always with a certain restraint and forbearance, because they were meant for the purpose of bringing him to reason. Thirty years of patience on his part had led her to believe that he would never carry retaliation beyond assassination plots. At last, in his slow way, he had gathered up all his strength and essayed to crush her. Thenceforward she was a convert to Drake's doctrine that attack was the surest way of defence. She had still good reasons for devolving this work as much as possible on the private enterprise of her subjects. The burden fell on those who asked nothing better than to be allowed to bear it. Thus arose that system, or rather practice, of leaving national work to be executed by private enterprise, which has had so much to do with the building up of the British Empire. Private gain has been the mainspring of action. National defence and aggrandisement have been almost incidental results. With Elizabeth herself national and private aims could not be dissevered. The nation and she had but one purse. She was cheaply defending England, and she shared in the plunder.

The favourite cruising-ground of the English adventurers was off the Azores, where the Spanish treasure fleets always halted for fresh water and provisions, on their way to Europe. Some of these expeditions were on a large scale. But they were not so successful or profitable, in proportion to their size, as the smaller ventures of Drake and Hawkins earlier in the reign. The Spaniards were everywhere on the alert. The harbours of the New World, which formerly lay in careless security, were put into a state of defence. Treasure fleets made their voyages with more caution. "Not a grain of gold, silver, or pearl, but what must be got through the fire." The day of great prizes was gone by.

Two of these expeditions are distinguished by their importance. The first was a joint-stock venture of Drake and Norris—the foremost sailor and the foremost soldier among Englishmen of that day—in the year after the great Armada (April 1589). They and some private backers found most of the capital. The Queen contributed six royal ships and £20,000. This fleet carried no less than 11,000 soldiers, for the aim was to wrest Portugal from the Spaniard and set up Don Antonio, a representative of the dethroned dynasty.

Stopping on their way at Corunna, they took the lower town, destroyed large stores, and defeated in the field a much superior force marching to the relief of the place. Norris mined and breached the walls of the upper town; but the storming parties having been repulsed with great loss, the army re-embarked and pursued its voyage. Landing at Peniché, Norris marched fifty miles by Vimiero and Torres Vedras, names famous afterwards in the military annals of England, and on the seventh day arrived before Lisbon. But he had no battering train; for Drake, who had brought the fleet round to the mouth of the Tagus, judged it dangerous to enter the river. Nor did the Portuguese rise, as had been hoped. The army therefore, marching through the suburbs of Lisbon, rejoined the fleet at Cascaes, and proceeded to Vigo. That town was burnt, and the surrounding country plundered. This was the last exploit of the expedition. Great loss and dishonour had been inflicted on Spain; but no less than half of the soldiers and sailors had perished by disease; and the booty, though said to have been large, was a disappointment to the survivors.

The other great expedition was in 1596. The capture of Calais in April of that year by the Spaniards, had renewed the alarm of invasion, and it was determined to meet the danger at a distance from home. A great fleet, with 6000 soldiers on board, commanded by Essex and Howard of Effingham sailed straight to Cadiz, the principal port and arsenal of Spain. The harbour was forced by the fleet, the town and castle stormed by the army, several men-of-war taken or destroyed, a large merchant-fleet burnt, together with an immense quantity of stores and merchandise; the total value being estimated at twenty millions of ducats. This was by far the heaviest blow inflicted by England upon Spain during the reign, and was so regarded in Europe; for though the great Armada had been signally defeated by the English fleet, its subsequent destruction was due to the winds and waves. Essex was vehemently desirous to hold Cadiz; but Effingham and the Council of War appointed by the Queen would not hear of it. The expedition accordingly returned home, having effectually relieved England from the fear of invasion. The burning of Penzance by four Spanish galleys (1595) was not much to set against these great successes.

One reason for the comparative impunity with which the English assailed the unwieldy empire of Philip was the insane pursuit of the French crown, to which he devoted all his resources after the murder of Henry III. In 1598, with one foot in the grave, and no longer able to conceal from himself that, with the exception of the conquest of Portugal, all the ambitious schemes of his life had failed, he was fain to conclude the peace of Vervins with Henry IV. Henry was ready to insist that England and the United Provinces should be comprehended in the treaty. Philip offered terms which Elizabeth would have welcomed ten years earlier. He proposed that the whole of the Low Countries should be constituted a separate sovereignty under his son-in-law the Archduke Albert. The Dutch, who were prospering in war as well as in trade, scouted the offer. English feeling was divided. There was a war-party headed by Essex and Raleigh, personally bitter enemies, but both athirst for glory, conquest, and empire, believing in no right but that of the strongest, greedy for wealth, and disdaining the slower, more laborious, and more legitimate modes of acquiring it. They were tired of campaigning it in France and the Low Countries, where hard knocks and beggarly plunder were all that a soldier had to look to. They proposed to carry a great English army across the Atlantic, to occupy permanently the isthmus of Panama, and from that central position to wrestle with the Spaniard for the trade and plunder of the New World. The peace party held that these ambitious schemes would bring no profit except possibly to a few individuals; that the treasury would be exhausted and the country irritated by taxation and the pressing of soldiers; that to re-establish the old commercial intercourse with Spain would be more reputable and attended with more solid advantage to the nation at large ; and finally, that the English arms would be much better employed in a thorough conquest of Ireland. These were the views of Burghley; and they were strongly supported by Buckhurst, the best of the younger statesmen who now surrounded Elizabeth.

Elizabeth always encouraged her ministers to speak their minds; but, as Buckhurst said on this occasion, "when they have done their extreme duty she wills what she wills." She determined to maintain the treaty of 1585 with the Dutch; but she took the opportunity of getting it amended in such a way as to throw upon them a larger share of the expenses of the war, and to provide more definitely for the ultimate repayment of her advances.

We have seen that three years before the Armada Elizabeth had lost the French alliance, which had till then been the key-stone of her policy. Since then, though aware that Henry III. wished her well, and that he would thwart the Spanish faction as much as he dared, she had not been able to count on him. He might at any moment be pushed by Guise into an attack on England, either with or without the concurrence of Spain. The accession, therefore, of Henry IV. afforded her great relief. In him she had a sure ally. It is true that, like her other allies the Dutch, he was more in a condition to require help than to afford it. But the more work she provided for Philip in Holland or France, the safer England would be. The armies of the Holy League might be formidable to Henry; but as long as he could hold them at bay they were not dangerous to England. She had never quite got over her scruple about helping the Dutch against their lawful sovereign. But Henry IV. was the legitimate King of France, and she could heartily aid him to put down his rebels. From 2000 to 5000 English troops were therefore constantly serving in France down to the peace of Vervins.

Philip, in defiance of the Salic law, claimed the crown of France for his daughter in right of her mother, who was a sister of Henry III. To Brittany he alleged that she had a special claim, as being descended from Anne of Brittany, which the Bourbons were not. Brittany, therefore, he invaded at once by sea. Elizabeth, alarmed by the proximity of this Spanish force, desired that her troops in France should be employed in expelling it, and that they should be vigorously supported by Henry IV. Henry, on the other hand, was always drawing away the English to serve his more pressing needs in other parts of France. This brought upon him many harsh rebukes and threats from the English Queen. But she had, for the first time, met her match. He judged, and rightly, that she would not desert him. So, with oft-repeated apologies, light promises, and well-turned compliments, he just went on doing what suited him best, getting all the fighting he could out of the English, and airily eluding Elizabeth's repeated demands for some coast town, which could be held, like Brill and Flushing, as a security for her heavy subsidies.

When Henry was reconciled to the Catholic Church, Elizabeth went through the form of expressing surprise and regret at a step which she must have long expected, and must have felt to be wise (1593). Her alliance with Henry was not shaken. It was drawn even closer by a new treaty, each sovereign engaging not to make peace without the consent of the other. This engagement did not prevent Henry from concluding the separate peace of Vervins five years later, when he judged that his interest required it (1598). Elizabeth's dissatisfaction was, this time, genuine enough. But Henry was no longer her protégé, a homeless, landless, penniless king, depending on English subsidies, roaming over the realm he called his own with a few thousands, or sometimes hundreds, of undisciplined cavaliers, who gathered and dispersed at their own pleasure. He was master of a re-united France, and could no longer be either patronised or threatened. Elizabeth might expostulate, and declare that "if there was such a sin as that against the Holy

Ghost it must needs be ingratitude:" gratitude was a sentiment to which she was as much a stranger as Henry. The only difference between them was the national one: the Englishwoman preached; the Frenchman mocked. What made her so sore was that he had, so to speak, stolen her policy from her. His predecessor had always suspected her—and with good reason—of intending "to draw her neck out of the collar" if once she could induce him to undertake a joint war. The joint war had at length been undertaken by Henry IV., and it was he who had managed to slip out of it first, while Elizabeth, who longed for peace, was obliged to stand by the Dutch.

The two sovereigns, however, knew their own interests too well to quarrel. Henry gave Elizabeth to understand that his designs against Spain had undergone no change; he was only halting for breath; he would help the Dutch underhand—just what she used to say to Henry III. She had now to deal with a French King as sagacious as herself, and a great deal more prompt and vigorous in action; not the man to be made a cat's-paw by any one. She had to accept him as a partner, if not on her own terms, then on his. Both sovereigns were thoroughly veracious—in Carlyle's sense of the word. That is to say, their policy was determined not by passion, or vanity, or sentiment of any kind, but by enlightened self-interest, and was therefore calculable by those who knew how to calculate.

CHAPTER XI

DOMESTIC AFFAIRS: 1588-1601

IT was a boast of Elizabeth that when once her servants were chosen she did not lightly displace them. Difference of opinion from their mistress, or from one another, did not involve resignation or dismissal, because, though they were free to speak their minds, all had to carry out with fidelity and even zeal, whatever policy the Queen prescribed. This condition they accepted; not only the astute and compliant Burghley, but the more eager and opinionated Walsingham; and therefore they had practically a life-tenure of office. Soon after the Armada the first generation of them began to disappear. Bacon, Sussex, and Bedford were already gone. Leicester died in 1588; his brother Warwick, and Mildmay in 1589; Walsingham and Randolph in 1591; Hatton in 1592; Grey de Wilton in 1593; Knollys and Hunsdon in 1596. Of the trusty servants with whom she began her reign, Burghley alone remained. The leading men of the new generation were Robert Cecil, the Treasurer's second son, trained to business under his father's eye, and of qualities similar, though inferior; Nottingham (formerly Howard of Effingham), a straightforward man of no great ability, but acceptable to the Queen for his father's services and his own (and not the less so for his fine presence); the accomplished Buckhurst; the brilliant Raleigh; and, younger than the rest, Essex. The last was the son of a man much favoured by Elizabeth. Leicester was his step-father, Knollys his grandfather, Hunsdon his great-uncle, Walsingham his father-in-law, Burghley his guardian. Ardent, impulsive, presumptuous, a warm friend, a rancorous enemy, profuse in expense, lawless in his amours, jealous of his equals, brooking no superior, impatient of all rule or order that delayed him from leaping at once to the highest place,—he was possessed with a most exaggerated notion of his own capacity, which appears to have been only moderate. As the ward of Burghley he had been much in the company of his future enemy, Robert Cecil, whose sly prim ways were most unlike his own. The contrast did him no harm with the public, to whom the younger man was a Tom Jones and the elder a Blifil. Two vastly abler men, Francis Bacon and Raleigh, less advantageously placed, but unhampered with any scruples, were busily trying to profit by the all-pervading animosity of Cecil and Essex.

Belonging, as Essex did by his connections, to the inner circle who stood closest to Elizabeth, it was natural that she should take an interest in him, and give him opportunities for turning his showy qualities to account. In 1586 he was sent to the Low Countries as general of cavalry under his step-father, Leicester. He distinguished himself by his fiery valour in the expeditions to Spain, and as commander of the English army in France, though he does not seem to have had any real military talent. But Elizabeth's regard for him was soon shaken by his presumptuous and unruly behaviour. When he fought a duel with Sir Charles Blount because she had conferred some favour on the latter, she swore "by God's death it were fitting some one should take him down and teach him better manners, or there were no rule with him." He displeased her by his quarrels with Cecil and Effingham, and his discontented grumbling. She was highly dissatisfied with his management of the Azores expedition in 1597. In July 1598, at a meeting of the Council, she was provoked by his insolence to strike him; and though after three months he obtained his pardon, he never regained her favour.

It was at this time that Burghley died (August 4), in his seventy-eighth year. Elizabeth, though she could call him "a froward old fool" about a trifling matter (March 1596), could not but feel that much was changed when she lost the able and faithful servant who had worked with her for forty years. "She seemeth to take it very grievously, shedding of tears and separating herself from all company." Buckhurst was the new Treasurer.

Essex had for some time cast his eyes on Ireland as a field where glory and power might be won. There can be little doubt that he was already speculating on the advantage that the possession of an army might give him in any difficulty with his rivals or with the Queen herself. Cecil perfidiously advocated his appointment to a post which had been the grave of so many reputations. The Queen at length consented, though reluctantly. Essex was a popular favourite. He had managed—it is not very clear how—to win the confidence of both Puritans and Papists. The general belief was that, for the first time since she had mounted the throne, Elizabeth was afraid of one of her subjects.

During the whole of the reign Ireland had been a cause of trouble and anxiety. Elizabeth's treatment of that unhappy country was not more creditable or successful than that of other English statesmen before and after her. There was the same absence of any systematic policy steadily carried out, the same wearisome and disreputable alternation between bursts of savage repression and intervals of pusillanimity, concession, and neglect. In the competition of the various departments of the public service for attention and expenditure, Ireland generally came last. All other needs had to be served first whether at home or abroad.

In the early years of the reign the chief trouble lay in Ulster, then the most purely Celtic part of Ireland, and practically untouched by English conquest. Twice, in her weariness of the struggle with Shan O'Neill, Elizabeth conceded to him something like a subkingship of Ulster in return for his nominal submission. In the end he was beaten, and his head was fixed on the walls of Dublin Castle (1566). But nothing further was done to anglicise Ulster. During the attempt of the Devonshire adventurers to colonise South Munster (1569-71), and the consequent rebellion, the northern province remained an unconcerned spectator. Nor did it join in the great Desmond rising (1579-83), which, with the insurrection of the Catholic lords of the Pale and the landing of the Pope's Italians at Smerwick, was the Irish branch of the threefold attack on Elizabeth directed by Gregory XIII. The attempt of the elder Essex to colonise Antrim (1573-75) was a disastrous failure, and Ulster still remained practically independent of the Dublin Government.

The most successful Deputy of the reign was Perrot (1584-87), a valiant soldier and strict ruler, who, after long experience in the Irish wars, had come to the conclusion that what Ireland most wanted was justice. The native chiefs, released from the constant dread of spoliation, and finding that English encroachment was repressed as inflexibly as Irish disorder, became quiet and friendly. But this system did not suit the dominant race. The Deputy was accused to the Queen of seeking to betray the country to the Irish and the Spaniard. Recalled, and put upon his trial for treason, he was found guilty on suborned evidence, and sentenced to death. It is usually said that his real offence was some disrespectful language about the Queen, which he confessed. But it seems that she forbore to take his life precisely because she would not have it thought that she was influenced by personal resentment.

His successor, Fitzwilliam, was a Deputy of the old sort—greedy, violent, careless of consequences, and always acting on the principle that, as against an Englishman, a Celt had no rights. The execution of MacMahon in Monaghan, and the confiscation of his lands on a trivial pretext, alarmed the North. Ulster had not been bled white like the rest of Ireland. The O'Neills had a nephew of their old hero Shan for their chief, who had been brought up at the English Court and made Earl of Tyrone by Elizabeth. An educated and remarkably able man, he had none of his uncle's illusions. He clung to his ancestral rights and dignity, but he hoped to preserve them by zealously discharging his obligations as a vassal of the Queen. He served in the war against Desmond, and exerted himself to maintain order in Ulster. But he had no mind to sink into the position of a mere dignified land-owner like the English nobles; nor indeed, under such a Deputy as Fitzwilliam, was he likely to preserve even his lands if he lost his power. Rather than that, he determined to enter into what he knew was a most unequal struggle, on the off-chance of pulling through by help from Spain. It is clear that he was driven into rebellion against his inclination. But when he had once drawn the sword he maintained the struggle against one Deputy after another with wonderful tenacity and resource. For the first time in Irish history, the rebel forces were disciplined and armed like those of the crown, and stood up to them in equal numbers on equal terms. At length, in August 1598, Tyrone inflicted upon Sir Henry Bagnall near Armagh the severest defeat that the English had ever suffered in Ireland; slaying 1500 of his men, and capturing all his artillery and baggage. Insurrections at once broke out all over Ireland.

This was the situation with which Essex undertook to deal. He had loudly blamed other•Deputies for

not vigorously attacking Tyrone in his own country.
Vigour was the one military quality which he himself
possessed. He went with the title of Lieutenant and
Governor-General, and with extraordinary powers, at
the head of 21,000 men—such an army as had never
been sent to Ireland (April 1599). The Queen,
who trembled at the expense, and did not wish to see
any of her nobles, least of all Essex, permanently
established in a great military command, enjoined him
to push at once into Ulster, as he had himself proposed, and finish the war. Instead of doing this, he
went south into districts that had been depopulated
and desolated by the savage warfare of the last thirty
years. Even here he met with discreditable reverses.
When he got back to Dublin (July) his army was
reduced by disease and desertion to less than 5000
men. Disregarding the Queen's express prohibition,
he made his friend Southampton General of horse.
When she censured his bad management, he replied
with impertinent complaints about the favour she was
showing to Cecil, Raleigh, and Cobham, and began to
consult with his friends about carrying selected troops
over to England to remove them. Rumours of his
intention to return reached the Queen. "We do
charge you," she wrote, "as you tender our pleasure,
that you adventure not to come out of that kingdom."
He declared that he could not invade Ulster without
reinforcements. They were sent, and at length he
marched into Louth (September). There he was met
by Tyrone, who, in an interview, completely twisted
him round his finger, and obtained a cessation of arms
and the promise of concessions amounting to what

would now be called Home Rule. A few days later, on receipt of an angry letter from the Queen forbidding him to grant any terms without her permission, he deserted his post and hurried to England. The first notice Elizabeth received of this astounding piece of insubordination was his still more astounding incursion into her bedroom, all muddy from his ride, before she was completely dressed (September 28, 1599).

Elizabeth seems to have been so much taken aback by the Earl's unparalleled presumption, that she did not blaze out as might have been expected. She gave him audience an hour or two later, and heard what he had to say. Probably he adopted an injured tone as usual, and inveighed against "that knave Raleigh" and "that sycophant Cobham." But his insubordination had been gross, and no talking could make it anything else. It was more dangerous than Leicester's disobedience in 1586, because it came from a vastly more dangerous person. The same afternoon the Queen referred the matter to the Council. Essex was put under arrest, and never saw her again. The more she reflected, the more indignant and alarmed she became. "By God's son," she said to Harington, "I am no Queen; this man is above me." After a delay of nine months, occasioned by his illness, the fallen favourite was brought before a special Commission on the charge of contempt and disobedience, and sentenced to be suspended from his offices and confined to his house during the Queen's pleasure (June 1600). In a few weeks he was released from arrest, but he could not obtain permission to appear at court, though he implored it in most abject letters.

There are persons who consider themselves to be intolerably wronged and persecuted if they cannot have precedence and power over their fellow-citizens. Essex was such a person. Instead of being thankful that he had escaped the punishment which under most sovereigns he would have suffered, he entered into criminal plots for coercing, if not overthrowing, the Queen. He urged the Scotch King to enforce the recognition of his title by arms. He tried to persuade Mountjoy, his successor in Ireland, to carry his army to Scotland to co-operate with James. These intrigues were not known to the Government. But it did not escape observation that he was collecting men of the sword in the neighbourhood of his house; that he was holding consultations with suspected nobles and gentlemen (some of whom were afterwards engaged in the Gunpowder Plot); that the Puritan clergy were preaching and praying for his cause; and that there was a certain ferment in the city. Essex was therefore summoned to attend before the Council. Instead of obeying, he flew to arms, with Lords Southampton, Rutland, Sandys, Cromwell, and Monteagle, and about 300 gentlemen. But the citizens of London did not respond to his appeal, and the insurrection was easily suppressed, less than a dozen persons being slain on both sides (February 8, 1601). A more senseless and profligate attempt to overthrow a good government it would be difficult to find in history. It was not dignified by any semblance of principle, and it would sufficiently stamp the character of its author, even if it stood alone as an evidence of his vanity, egotism, and want of common sense.

The trial and execution of the principal malefactor followed as a matter of course and without delay (February 25). It would have been scandalous to spare him. Elizabeth had once been fond of him, and had no reason to be ashamed of it. To talk of her "passion" and her "amorous inclination," as Hume and others have done, is revolting and malignant nonsense. It is creditable to old age when it can take pleasure in the unfolding of bright and promising youth. But royal favour was not good for such a man as Essex. It developed the worst features in his showy but faulty character. As he steadily deteriorated, her regard cooled; but so much of it remained that she tried to amend him by chastisement, "*ad correctionem*," as she said, "*non ad ruinam.*" She had long before warned him that, though she had put up with much disrespect to her person, he must not touch her sceptre, or he would be dealt with according to the law of England. She was as good as her word, and, though the memory of it was painful to her, there is not the smallest evidence that she ever repented of having allowed the law to take its course.[1] Only three of the accomplices of Essex were punished capitally. The five peers, none of them powerful or formidable, experienced Elizabeth's accustomed clemency.

It has been suggested by an admirer of Essex that he failed in Ireland because his "sensitively attuned nature" shrank from the systematic desolation and starvation afterwards employed by his successor. No

---

[1] The story of the ring, said to have been intercepted by Lady Nottingham, has been shown to be unworthy of belief. See Ranke, *History of England*, vol. i. p. 352; transl.

evidence is offered for this suggestion. In a letter to the Queen (June 25, 1599) he advocates "burning and spoiling the country *in all places*," which method "shall starve the rebels in one year." This course Mountjoy carried out. With means far inferior to those of Essex, and notwithstanding the landing of 3000 Spaniards at Kinsale (September 1601), he was the first Englishman who completely subdued Ireland. Tyrone surrendered a few days before the Queen's death.

Little has been said in these pages about parliamentary proceedings. The real history of the reign does not lie there. The country was governed wholly by the Queen, with the advice of her Council, and not at all by Parliament. \In the forty-five years of her reign there were only thirteen sessions of Parliament. The functions of Parliament were to vote grants of money when the ordinary revenues of the crown were insufficient, and to make laws. Its right in these matters was unquestioned. If the Queen had never wanted subsidies or penal laws against her political and religious opponents (of other laws she often said there were more than enough already), it would never have been summoned at all; nor is there any reason to suppose that the country would have complained as long as it was governed with prudence and success. In fact, to do without Parliaments was distinctly popular, because it meant doing without subsidies.

In the thirty years preceding the Armada—the sessions of Parliament being nine—Elizabeth applied for only eight subsidies, and of one of them a portion was remitted. By her economy she not only defrayed the expenses of government out of the ordinary revenue, which, at the end of the reign was about £300,000 a year, but paid off old debts. It was not till the twenty-fourth year of her reign that she discharged the last of her father's debts, up to which time she had been paying interest on it. Subsequently she even accumulated a small reserve, which, as she told Parliament, was a most necessary thing if she was not to be driven to borrow on sudden emergency. But this reserve vanished immediately she became involved in the great war with Spain; and during the last fifteen years of her life, although she received twelve subsidies, she was always in difficulty for money. She had to sell crown lands to the value of £372,000. Parliament, which had voted the usual single subsidies without complaint, grumbled and pretended poverty when she asked for three and even four.[1] Bacon's famous outburst (1593) about gentlemen having to sell their plate and farmers their brass pots to pay the tax, was a piece of claptrap. The nation was, relatively to former times, rolling in wealth. But the old belief had still considerable strength—that government being the affair of the King, not of his subjects, he should provide for its expenses out of his hereditary income, just as they paid their private expenses out of their private incomes; that he had no more claim to dip into their pockets than they had to dip into his; and that a subsidy, as its name imports, was an occasional and extraordinary assistance furnished as a matter not of duty but of good-will.

[1] The increase was not so great as it appears. A subsidy with two tenths and fifteenths in the thirteenth year of the reign yielded £175,000; in the forty-third only £134,000.

This might have been healthy doctrine when kings were campaigning on the Continent for personal or dynastic objects. It was out of place when a large expenditure was indispensable for the interests and safety of the country. The grumbling, therefore, about taxation towards the end of the reign was unreasonable and discreditable to the grumblers. The Queen met them with her usual good sense. She explained to them—though, as she correctly said, she was under no constitutional obligation to do so—how the money went, what she had spent on the Spanish war, on Ireland, and in loans to the Dutch and the French King. The plea was unanswerable. Her private expenditure was on a very modest scale. In particular she had never indulged in that besetting and costly sin of princes, palace-building; and this at a time when the noble mansions which still testify to the wealth of the England of that day were rising in every county. Her only extravagance was dress. Some have carped at her collection of jewelry. But jewels, like the silver balustrades of Frederick William I., were a mode of hoarding, and in her later years she reconverted jewels into money to meet the expenses of the State. Modern writers, who so airily blame her for not subsidising more liberally her Scotch, Dutch, and French allies, would find it difficult, if they condescended to particulars, to explain how she was able to give them as much money as she did.

It is common to make much of the debate on monopolies in the last Parliament of Elizabeth (1601), as showing the rise of a spirit of resistance to the royal prerogative. I do not think that the report of that debate would convey such an impression to any one reading it without preconceived views. None of the speakers contested the prerogative. They only complained that it was being exercised in a way prejudicial to the public interest. If the monopolies had been unimportant, or if the patentees had used their privilege less greedily, there would evidently have been no complaint as to the principle involved. No course of action was decided on, because the Queen intervened by a message in which she stated that she had not been aware of the abuses prevailing, that she was as indignant at them as Parliament could be, and that she would put a stop, not to monopolies, but to such as were injurious. With this message the House of Commons was more than satisfied. As a matter of fact monopolies went on till dealt with by the declaratory statute in the twenty-first year of James I.

If the last Tudor handed down the English Constitution to the first Stuart as she had received it from her predecessors, unchanged either in theory or practice, it was far otherwise with the English Church. There are two conflicting views as to the historical position of the Church in this country. According to one it was, all through the Middle Age, National as well as Catholic. The changes which took place at the Reformation made no difference in that respect, and involved no break in its continuity. It is not a Protestant Church. It is still National and still Catholic, resting on precisely the same foundations, and existing by the same title as it did in the days of Dunstan and Becket. According to the other view, the epithets National and Catholic are contradictory. A Church which undergoes radical changes of government, worship, and doctrine is no longer the same Church but a new one, and must be held to have been established by the authority which prescribed these changes, which, in this case, was the Queen and Parliament. The word "Protestant" was avoided in its formularies to make conformity easier for Catholics; but it is a Protestant Church all the same. Whichever of these views is nearer to the truth, it cannot be denied that, by the legislation of Elizabeth the English Church became—what it was not in the Middle Age—a spiritual organisation entirely dependent on the State. This it remains still; the supremacy having been virtually transferred from the crown to Parliament in the next century. I shall not venture to inquire how far this condition of dependence has affected its ability and inclination to perform the part of a true spiritual power. It is enough to say that no act of will on the part of any English statesman has had such important and lasting consequences, for good or for evil, as the decision of Elizabeth to make the Church of England what it is.

We have seen that the government and worship of the Church were established by Act of Parliament in 1559, and its doctrines in 1571. But when once Elizabeth had placed her ecclesiastical powers beyond dispute, by obtaining statutory sanction for them, she allowed no further interference by Parliament. All its attempts, even at mere discussion of ecclesiastical matters, she peremptorily suppressed. She supplied any further legislation that was needed by virtue of her supremacy, and she exercised her ecclesiastical government by the Court of High Commission. The new Anglican model was acquiesced in by the majority of the nation. But it had, at first, no hearty support except from the Government. The earnest religionists were either Catholics or Puritans. The object of Elizabeth was to compel these two extreme parties to outward conformity of worship. What their real beliefs were she did not care.

The large majority of the Catholics showed a loyal and patriotic spirit at the time of the Armada. But they were not treated with confidence by the Government. Great numbers of them were imprisoned or confined in the houses of Protestant gentlemen, by way of precaution, when the Armada was approaching. No Catholic, I believe, was intrusted with any command either by land or sea; and after the danger was over, the persecution, in all its forms, became sharper than ever. There was the less reason for this, inasmuch as it was no secret that the secular priests and the great majority of the English Catholics had become bitterly hostile to the small Jesuitical faction whose treasonable conspiracies had brought so much trouble on their loyal co-religionists.

The term "Puritan" is used loosely, though conveniently, to designate several shades of belief. By far the larger number of those to whom it is applied were, and meant to remain, members of the Established Church. They objected to certain ceremonies and vestments. They hoped to procure the abolition of these, and, in the meantime, evaded them when they could. They were what would now be called the Evangelical or Low Church party. They held Calvin's distinctive doctrines on predestination, as indeed did most of the bishops; but though preferring his Presbyterian organisation, or something like it, they did not treat it as essential. They were broadly distinguished from the Brownists or Independents, then an insignificant minority, who held each congregation to be a church, and therefore protested against the establishment of any national church.

Though Elizabeth persecuted the Catholics with a severity steadily increasing in proportion as they became less numerous and formidable, she remained to the last anxious to make conformity easy for them. This was her reason for so obstinately refusing the concessions in the matter of ritual and vestments—trifling as they appear to the modern mind—which would have satisfied almost the whole of the Puritan party. This policy (for policy it assuredly was rather than conviction), which drove the most earnest Protestants into an attitude of opposition destined in the next two reigns to have such serious consequences, has been severely censured. But there can be no question that it did answer the purpose she had in view, which for the moment was most important. It did induce great numbers of Catholics to conform. She avoided a civil war in her own time between Catholics and Anglicans at the price of a civil war later on between Anglicans and Puritans. Looking at the great drama as a whole, perhaps the Puritans of the Great Rebellion might congratulate themselves on the part that Elizabeth chose to play in its earlier acts. It cannot be doubted that a civil war in the sixteenth century between Catholics and Protestants would have been waged with far more ferocity than was displayed by either Cavaliers or Roundheads, and would have been attended with the horrors of foreign invasion. To conciliate the earnest religionists on both sides was impossible. Elizabeth chose the *via media*, and the successful equilibrium which she maintained during nearly half a century proves that she hit upon what in her own day was the true centre of gravity.

But while doing justice to Elizabeth's insight and prudence, we may not excuse her extreme severity to the nonconformists of either party. It was not necessary. It seems to have been even impolitic. It arose from her arbitrary temper—from a quality, that is to say, valuable in a ruler, but apt, in great rulers, to be somewhat in excess. I have condemned her persecution of the Catholics. Her persecution of the Protestant nonconformists was marked by even greater injustice. Against the Catholics it might at least be urged that their opinions logically led to disloyalty. But the Independents, Barrow, Greenwood, and Penry, were indisputably loyal men. They were put to death nominally for spreading writings which, contrary to common sense, were held to be seditious, but really for their religious opinions, which, in the case of the first two, were extracted from them by the interrogatories of Archbishop Whitgift, an Inquisitor as strenuous and merciless as Torquemada. Some of the Council, especially Burghley and Knollys, were strongly opposed to Whitgift's proceedings. It must therefore be assumed that he had the Queen's personal approval. She had committed herself to a struggle with intrepid and obstinate men. The crowded gaols were a visible demonstration that she could not compel them to submit; and to hang them all was out of the question. An Act was therefore passed in 1593, by which those who would not promise to attend church were to be banished the country. Thus most of the Independents were at last got rid of. The non-separatist Puritans, who aimed at less radical changes, and hoped to effect them, if not under their present sovereign, yet under her successor, kept on the windy side of the law, attending church once a month, and not entering till the service was nearly over. Thus, at the end of her reign, Elizabeth perhaps flattered herself that she was within measurable distance of religious uniformity.

CHAPTER XII

LAST YEARS AND DEATH: 1601-1603.

THE death of Mary Stuart did something to simplify parties in Scotland; and, if her son had possessed the qualities of a ruler, he would have had a better chance of reducing his kingdom to order than any of his predecessors, because a middle class was at length rising into importance. As far as knowledge and discernment went, he was an able politician, and on several occasions he showed not only skill in his combinations, but—what he is not generally credited with by those who study only his career in England — considerable energy and courage. But he was wanting in perseverance, and a slave to idle pleasures. He had always some favourite upon whom he lavished any money that came into his hands. What was needed in his own interest and that of his country was that he should exercise rigid economy, develop all the forces that made for order, ally himself with the burghs and lower barons, cultivate good relations with the Kirk, industriously attend to all the details of government, and seize every opportunity to humble the great nobles of whatever party or creed. Instead of this, he tried to maintain himself by balancing rival parties, and employing one nobleman to execute his vengeance on another. Instead of honestly and zealously seconding the policy of Elizabeth, and so deserving her confidence and support, which would have been of the utmost value to him, he tried to levy blackmail on her by coquetting with Spain and the Catholics.

Elizabeth is accused of deliberately encouraging Scottish factions in order to keep the northern kingdom weak. She certainly supported Stewart, Earl of Bothwell, a turbulent and unprincipled man, while he was the antagonist of the Catholic nobles who were inviting the Spaniard. But it is plain that she desired nothing so much as to see James crush all aristocratic disorder, and make himself master of his kingdom. Her exhortations to him on this subject are full of wisdom, and expressed in most stirring language. But they only produced petitions for money. Notwithstanding her own difficulties, she long allowed him £3000 a year, which, in 1600, was increased to £6000. But ten times that amount would have done him no good, because he would immediately have squandered it.

As Elizabeth grew old, James naturally became absorbed in the prospect of his succession to the English crown. All Scotchmen shared his eagerness. In England, feeling was almost unanimous in his favour, though some of the Catholics continued to talk of the Infanta or Arabella Stuart the niece of Darnley. By teasing Elizabeth to recognise his title, intriguing with her courtiers, and calling on his own subjects to furnish him with the means of asserting his rights, James irritated the English Queen. But she had always intended that he should succeed her, and she did nothing to prejudice his claim.

The two leading men at the English court—Cecil and Raleigh—who had been united in their hostility to Essex, were now secretly competing for the favour of James. Each warned the Scottish King against the other, and represented himself as the only trustworthy adviser. Cecil, from his confidential relations with the Queen, had the most difficult game to play, and it was not till her health was evidently failing that he ventured to open private communications with James. Even then he did not dare to correspond with him directly, but it was understood that everything written by Lord Henry Howard (brother of the last Duke of Norfolk) was to be taken as written by Cecil. To make up for his previous backwardness, he lent James £10,000—a pledge of fidelity which it was out of his rival's power to emulate.

The long career of Elizabeth was now drawing to its close. Her sun might seem to be going down in calm splendour. She had triumphed over all her enemies. She might say with Virgil's heroine—

"Vixi, et quem dederat cursum fortuna, peregi;
Et nunc magna mei sub terras ibit imago."

The mighty Philip had gone to his grave five years before her (1598), a beaten man, having failed in Holland, failed in France, failed against England. Of the three great champions who withstood him, Elizabeth, if not the most distinguished by high qualities, had yet, perhaps, laid up store of calm satisfaction. Europe from the retrograde tyranny. The glorious resistance of William of Orange, thanks only sixteen years (1568-84). That of Henry, diet, can hardly be said to have had any European importance before his accession to the French throne, from which date to the peace of Vervins and the death of Philip is a period of nine years (1589-98). But the whole of Elizabeth's long reign was spent in abating the power of Spain. It was the persistent, never-relaxing pressure from an unassailable enemy which wore out Philip, as it afterwards wore out Bonaparte. Elizabeth had found England weak and distracted: she was leaving it united and powerful. Nor was she of those to whom their due meed of praise is denied during life, and accorded only by the tardy justice of posterity. Her wisdom and courage were the admiration not of her own people alone, but of all Europe. "Her very enemies," says a French historian, "proclaimed her the most glorious and fortunate of all women who ever wore a crown." From the point of view of public life, little or nothing was wanting—so Bacon thought—to fill up the full measure of her felicity.

Yet it seems that the last months of her life were clouded by melancholy, and deformed by a querulous ill-temper. Some have suggested that she suffered from remorse for her severity to Essex; others that she felt herself out of sympathy with the Puritan tendencies of the time. It is not necessary to resort to these unfounded or far-fetched suppositions to account for her gloom. If we turn from her public subjects to furnish him. No situation could be more his rights, James in Honour and obedience, indeed, she had always had her. But that which also should and should any old age, love and troops of friends, she might not look to have. Near relations she had none. Alone she had chosen to live, and alone she must die. As her time approached, she was haunted by the consciousness that, among all those who treated her with so much reverence, there was not one who had any reason to be attached to her or to care that her life should be prolonged. Those who have not loved when they were young must not expect to find love when they are old. While health and strength remained, she had tasted the satisfaction of living her own life and playing the great game of politics, for which she was exceptionally gifted. But to a woman who has passed through life without knowing what it is to love or be loved, who has no memory of even an unrequited affection to feed on, who has never shared a husband's joys and sorrows, never borne the sweet burden of maternity, never suckled babe or rocked cradle, who must finish her journey alone, sitting in the solemn twilight before the last dark hour uncared for and uncaring, without the cheer of children or the varied interests that gather round the family—to such a one, what avails it that she has tasted the excitement of public life, that she has borne a share in politics or business—what even that her aims have been high or that she has done the State some service, if she has renounced the crown of womanhood, and turned from their appointed use those numbered years within which the female heart can find present joy and lay up store of calm satisfaction for declining age?

Elizabeth had always enjoyed good health, thanks to her "exact temperance both as to wine and diet, which, she used to say, was the noblest part of physic," and her active habits. In capacity for resisting bodily fatigue and freedom from nervous ailments, she was like a man. It was not till the beginning of 1602 that those about her noticed any signs of failing strength. She still went on hunting and dancing. In dancing she excelled, and she kept it up for exercise, as many an old man keeps up his skating or tennis without being exposed to ill-natured remarks. In December 1602 her godson Harington, an amusing person, whose company she enjoyed, found her "in most pitiable state," both in body and mind. "She held in her hand a golden cup which she often put to her lips; but in sooth her heart seemeth too full to lack more filling." He read her some verses he had written, "whereat she smiled once," but said, "When thou dost feel creeping Time at thy gate, these fooleries will please thee less. I am past my relish for such matters. Thou seest my bodily meat doth not suit me well. I have eaten but one ill-tasted cake since yesternight." Harington hastened to send a present to the King of Scots, with the inscription, "*Domine memento mei cum veneris in regnum.*"

In the same month Robert Carey, son of her cousin Lord Hunsdon, visited her, and professed to think her looking well. "No, Robin," she said, "I am not well," and then "discoursed of her indisposition, and that her heart had been sad and heavy for ten or twelve days, and in her discourse she fetched not so few as forty or fifty great sighs. . . . Hereupon I wrote to the King of Scots."[1] Her melancholy was not caused by any weakening of her mind. A long letter to James, dated January 5, 1603, though hardly legible, is very vigorous and characteristic.

At the beginning of March 1603 she became much worse. There was some disease of the throat, attended with swelling and a distressing formation of phlegm, which made speaking difficult. The only relatives about her were Robert Carey and his sister Lady Scrope, watching keenly that they might be the first to inform James of her death. She could not be brought by any of her Council to take food or go to bed. When in bed she had been troubled by a visual illusion; "she saw her body exceedingly lean and fearful in a light of fire." At last Nottingham, the Admiral, who was mourning the recent death of his wife, was sent for. He was a second cousin of Anne Boleyn, and was the one person to whom the dying Queen seemed to cling with some trust. He induced her to take some broth. "For any of the rest," says her maid-of-honour, Mistress Southwell, "she would not answer them to any question, but said softly to my Lord Admiral's earnest persuasions that if he knew what she had seen in her bed he would not persuade

---

[1] Elizabeth made large use of the courage and fidelity of her kinsmen on the Boleyn side, but she did little to advance them either in rank or wealth. Hunsdon had set his heart on regaining the Boleyn Earldom of Wiltshire. When he was dying, Elizabeth brought the patent and robes of an earl, and laid them on his bed; but the choleric old man replied, "Madam, seeing you counted me not worthy of this honour while I was living, I count myself unworthy of it now I am dying."

her as he did. And Secretary Cecil, overhearing her, asked if her Majesty had seen any spirits; to which she said she scorned to answer him so idle a question. Then he told her how, to content the people, her Majesty must go to bed. To which she smiled, wonderfully contemning him, saying that the word *must* was not to be used to princes; and thereupon said, 'Little man, little man, if your father had lived ye [he?] durst not have said so much: but thou knowest I must die, and that maketh thee so presumptuous.' And presently commanding him and the rest to depart her chamber, willed my Lord Admiral to stay; to whom she shook her head, and with a pitiful voice said, 'My Lord, I am tied with a chain of iron about my neck.' He alleging her wonted courage to her, she replied, 'I am tied, and the case is altered with me.'" At last, "what by fair means," says Carey, "what by force, he got her to bed."

It was perfectly understood that she meant James to be her successor. The Admiral now told his colleagues that she had confided her intention to him just before her illness took a serious turn. Two years before, in conversation with Rosni, the minister of Henry IV., she had spoken of the approaching union of the Scotch and English crowns as a matter of course. But it was not till a few hours before her death that her councillors ventured to question her on the subject. They gave out that she indicated James by a sign; and this is also asserted by Carey, who, however, does not seem to have been present, though probably his sister was. Mistress Southwell seems to write as an eye-witness, but betrays a Catholic bias, which may cast some doubt on her testimony. "The Council sent to her the bishop of Canterbury and other of the prelates, upon sight of whom she was much offended, cholericly rating them, bidding them be packing, saying she was no atheist, but knew full well they were hedge-priests, and took it for an indignity that they should speak to her. Now being given over by all, and at the last gasp, keeping still her sense in everything and giving ever when she spoke apt answers, though she spake very seldom, having then a sore throat, she desired to wash it, that she might answer more freely to what the Council demanded; which was to know whom she would have king; but they, seeing her throat troubled her so much, desired her to hold up her finger when they named whom liked her. Whereupon they named the king of France, the king of Scotland, at which she never stirred. They named my lord Beauchamp,[1] whereto she said, 'I will have no rascal's son in my seat, but one worthy to be a king.' Hereupon instantly she died." (March 23, afternoon.)

It is certain, however, that she lived several hours after this characteristic outburst. Carey says that at six o'clock in the evening he went into her room with the Archbishop; that, though speechless, she showed by signs that she followed his prayers, and twice desired him to remain when he was going away. She died in the early hours of Thursday, March 24.

There have been many greater statesmen than Elizabeth. She was far from being an admirable type of womanhood. She does not, in my opinion, stand first even among female sovereigns, for I should put

[1] Son of Catherine Grey by the Earl of Hertford. "Rascal" at that time meant a person of low birth.

that able ruler and perfect woman, Isabella of Castile, above her. I admit, however, that such comparisons are apt to be unjust. Few rulers have had to contend with such formidable and complicated difficulties as the English Queen. Few have surmounted them so triumphantly. This is the criterion, and the sufficient criterion, which determines the judgment of practical men. Research, if applied with fairness and common sense, may perhaps modify, it can never set aside, the popular verdict. There are writers who have made the discovery that Elizabeth was a very poor ruler, selfish and wayward, shortsighted, easily duped, fainthearted, rash, miserly, wasteful, and swayed by the pettiest impulses of vanity, spite, and personal inclination. They have not explained, and never will, how it was that a woman with all these disqualifications for government should have ruled England with signal success for forty-four years. Statesmen are indebted to good luck occasionally, like other people. But when this explanation is offered again and again with dull regularity, we are compelled to say, with one who had at once the best opportunity and the highest capacity for estimating the greatness of Elizabeth : "It is not to closet penmen that we are to look for guidance in such a case; for men of that order being keen in style, poor in judgment, and partial in feeling, are no faithful witnesses as to the real passages of business. It is for ministers and great officers to judge of these things, and those who have handled the helm of government and been acquainted with the difficulties and mysteries of State business."[1]

[1] Bacon, *In felicem memoriam Elizabethæ*.

The judgment of those who have handled the helm of government is to be found in the words of her contemporary, the great Henry—"She was my other self:" and of a greater still in the next generation—"Queen Elizabeth of famous memory; we need not be ashamed to call her so!"[1]

[1] Carlyle, *Letters and Speeches of Oliver Cromwell*, Speech v.

APPENDIX

APPENDIX A.

SESSIONS OF PARLIAMENT IN THE REIGN OF ELIZABETH.

Parliament.	*Year of Elizabeth.*	*Began.*	*Prorogued.*	*Dissolved.*
I.	1st	25 Jan. 155$\frac{8}{9}$		8 May 1559
II.	5th	12 Jan. 156$\frac{2}{3}$	10 April 1563	
II. 2nd Sess.	8th and 9th	30 Sep. 1566	30 Dec. 1566	2 Jan. 156$\frac{6}{7}$
III.	13th	2 April 1571		29 May 1571
IV.	14th	8 May 1572	30 June 1572	
IV. 2nd Sess.	18th	8 Feb. 157$\frac{5}{6}$	15 Mar. 157$\frac{5}{6}$	
V. 3rd Sess.	23rd	16 Jan. 158$\frac{0}{1}$	18 Mar. 158$\frac{0}{1}$	19 April 1583
V.	27th and 28th	23 Nov. 1584*	29 Mar. 1585	14 Sep. 1586
VI.	28th and 29th	15 Oct. 1586*	29 Oct. 1586	23 Mar. 158$\frac{6}{7}$
VII.	31st	4 Feb. 158$\frac{8}{9}$		29 Mar. 1589
VIII.	35th	19 Feb. 159$\frac{2}{3}$		10 April 1593
IX.	39th	24 Oct. 1597*		9 Feb. 159$\frac{7}{8}$
X.	43rd	27 Oct. 1601		19 Dec. 1601

* Adjourned over Christmas Vacation.

APPENDIX B.

THE PRINCIPAL HOWARDS CONTEMPORARIES OF ELIZABETH.

2ND DUKE OF NORFOLK.[1]

- **3RD DUKE OF NORFOLK.[2]** — **EDMUND.** — **LADY BOLEYN.[9]** — **WILLIAM 1ST LORD HOWARD OF EFFINGHAM.[10]**
  - MARY.[4] EARL OF SURREY.[3] Q. CATHERINE HOWARD. Q. ANNE BOLEYN. CHARLES 2ND LORD EFFINGHAM.[11]
    - 4TH DUKE OF NORFOLK.[5] HENRY.[12]
      - EARL OF ARUNDEL.[6] LORD HOWARD[7] WILLIAM[8] OF WALDEN.
  - QUEEN ELIZABETH.

[1] As Earl of Surrey commanded at Flodden.
[2] Minister of Henry VIII.
[3] The Poet. Beheaded by Henry VIII.
[4] Married Duke of Richmond, natural son of Henry VIII.
[5] Beheaded by Elizabeth. Title forfeited.
[6] Earl of Arundel in right of his mother 1st wife of father. Died in Tower.
[7] Lord Walden in right of his mother 2nd wife of father.
[8] "Belted Will," married co-heiress of Lord Dacre of Naworth.
[9] Elizabeth Howard married Sir Thomas Boleyn created Earl of Wiltshire and Ormonde by Henry VIII.
[10] Lord Admiral. Created Lord Effingham by Mary.
[11] Lord Admiral. Commanded against Armada. Created Earl of Nottingham by Elizabeth.
[12] Created Earl of Northampton by James I.

APPENDIX C.

PRINCIPAL BOLEYN RELATIONS OF ELIZABETH.

```
                    SIR THOMAS BOLEYN¹=LADY ELIZABETH HOWARD.²
                                    │
        ┌───────────────────┬───────┴──────────┐
        │                   │                  │
  LORD ROCHFORD.³      QUEEN ANNE.        MARY=WILLIAM CAREY.
                            │                  │
                      QUEEN ELIZABETH.   ┌─────┴──────────────────────┐
                                         │                            │
                                   1ST LORD HUNSDON.⁴         CATHERINE=SIR FRANCIS
                                         │                              KNOLLYS.
        ┌────────────┬──────────┬────────┴────────┐                  │
        │            │          │                 │        ┌─────────┴──────────┐
  2ND LORD       ROBERT.⁵   LADY EFFINGHAM⁶   LADY SCROPE.  WALTER, EARL=LETTICE=EARL OF LEICESTER.
  HUNSDON.                  AND COUNTESS                    OF ESSEX.
                            OF NOTTINGHAM.                       │
                                                          ROBERT, EARL OF ESSEX⁷=FRANCES SIDNEY.⁸
```

¹ Created Earl of Wiltshire and Ormonde by Henry VIII.
² Daughter of 2nd Duke of Norfolk.
³ Beheaded by Henry VIII.
⁴ Elizabeth's Minister and General.
⁵ Carried news of Elizabeth's death to James; created by him Earl of Monmouth.
⁶ Said to have withheld Essex's ring from Elizabeth.
⁷ Beheaded by Elizabeth.
⁸ Daughter of Sir Francis Walsingham and widow of Sir Philip Sidney.

Printed by T. and A. CONSTABLE, Printers to Her Majesty,
at the Edinburgh University Press.

Messrs. MACMILLAN & CO.'S PUBLICATIONS.

Now Publishing. Crown 8vo. 2s. 6d. each.

TWELVE ENGLISH STATESMEN.

⁎ A Series of Short Biographies, not designed to be a complete roll of famous Statesmen, but to present in historic order the lives and work of those leading actors in our affairs who, by their direct influence, have left an abiding mark on the policy, the institutions, and the position of Great Britain among States.

WILLIAM THE CONQUEROR. By EDWARD A. FREEMAN, D.C.L., LL.D.
Times.—'Gives with great picturesqueness. . . . the dramatic incidents of a memorable career.'

HENRY II. By Mrs. J. R. Green.
Times.—'Delightfully real and readable.'

EDWARD I. By F. YORK POWELL. [In preparation.

HENRY VII. By JAMES GAIRDNER.
Athenæum.—'The best account of Henry VII. that has yet appeared.'

CARDINAL WOLSEY. By Professor M. CREIGHTON.
Saturday Review.—'Is exactly what one of a series of short biographies of English Statesmen ought to be.'

ELIZABETH. By E. S. BEESLY.

OLIVER CROMWELL. By FREDERIC HARRISON.
Times.—'Gives a wonderfully vivid picture of events.'

WILLIAM III. By H. D. TRAILL.

WALPOLE. By JOHN MORLEY.
World.—'The model of what history on such a scale should be.'

CHATHAM. By JOHN MORLEY. [In preparation.

PITT. By LORD ROSEBERY.
Times.—'There are abundant proofs in this brilliant and facsinating little book that Lord Rosebery possesses literary gifts of a very high order. . . . The style is terse, masculine, nervous, articulate, and clear; the grasp of circumstance and character is firm, penetrating, luminous, and unprejudiced; the judgment is broad, generous, humane, and scrupulously candid, even when it provokes dissent; and the whole book is irradiated with incessant flashes of genial and kindly humour, with frequent felicities of epigrammatic expression. . . . It is not only a luminous estimate of Pitt's character and policy, at once candid, sympathetic, and kindly; it is also a brilliant gallery of portraits, set in a background of broadly-sketched political landscape. The portrait of Fox, for example, is a masterpiece.'
Daily News.—'Requires no further recommendation than its own intrinsic merits. . . . It is in many respects, and those not the least essential, a model of what such a work should be. . . . By far the most powerful, because the most moderate and judicious defence of Pitt's whole career ever yet laid before the world.'

PEEL. By J. R. THURSFIELD.
Daily News.—'A model of what such a book should be. We can give it no higher praise than to say that it is worthy to rank with Mr. John Morley's *Walpole* in the same series.'

MACMILLAN AND CO., LONDON.

Messrs. MACMILLAN AND CO.'S PUBLICATIONS.

ENGLISH MEN OF ACTION SERIES.

Crown 8vo, cloth. 2s. 6d. each.

GENERAL GORDON. By Colonel Sir WILLIAM BUTLER.
Spectator.—'This is beyond all question the best of the narratives of the career of General Gordon that have yet been published.'

HENRY THE FIFTH. By the Rev. A. J. CHURCH.

LIVINGSTONE. By Mr. THOMAS HUGHES.
Spectator.—'The volume is an excellent instance of miniature biography.'

LORD LAWRENCE. By Sir RICHARD TEMPLE.
Leeds Mercury.—'A lucid, temperate, and impressive summary.'

WELLINGTON. By Mr. GEORGE HOOPER.
Scotsman.—'The story of the great Duke's life is admirably told by Mr. Hooper.

DAMPIER. By Mr. W. CLARK RUSSELL.
Athenæum.—'Mr. Clark Russell's practical knowledge of the sea enables him to discuss the seafaring life of two centuries ago with intelligence and vigour. As a commentary on Dampier's voyages this little book is among the best.'

MONK. By Mr. JULIAN CORBETT.
Saturday Review.—'Mr. Corbett indeed gives you the real man.'

STRAFFORD. By Mr. H. D. TRAILL.
Athenæum.—'A clear and accurate summary of Strafford's life, especially as regards his Irish government.'

WARREN HASTINGS. By Sir ALFRED LYALL.
Daily News.—'May be pronounced without hesitation as the final and decisive verdict of history on the conduct and career of Hastings.'

PETERBOROUGH. By Mr. W. STEBBING.
Saturday Review.—'An excellent piece of work.'

CAPTAIN COOK. By Mr. WALTER BESANT.
Scottish Leader.—'It is simply the best and most readable account of the great navigator yet published.'

SIR HENRY HAVELOCK. By Mr. ARCHIBALD FORBES.
Speaker.—'There is no lack of good writing in this book, and the narrative is sympathetic as well as spirited.'

CLIVE. By Colonel Sir CHARLES WILSON.
Times.—'Sir Charles Wilson, whose literary skill is unquestionable, does ample justice to a great and congenial theme.'

SIR CHARLES NAPIER. By Colonel Sir WILLIAM BUTLER.
Daily News.—'The "English Men of Action" series contains no volume more fascinating, both in matter and in style.'

WARWICK, THE KING-MAKER. By Mr. C. W. C. OMAN.
Anti-Jacobin.—'The most valuable of the excellent series to which it belongs... Beyond question the best book which has yet appeared on the Wars of the Roses.'
Glasgow Herald.—'One of the best and most discerning word-pictures of the Wars of the Two Roses to be found in the whole range of English literature.'

DRAKE. By Mr. JULIAN CORBETT.
Scottish Leader.—'Perhaps the most fascinating of all the fifteen that have so far appeared.... Written really with excellent judgment, in a breezy and buoyant style.'

RODNEY. By Mr. DAVID G. HANNAY.

MONTROSE. By Mr. MOWBRAY MORRIS.

And the undermentioned are in the Press or in Preparation:—

MARLBOROUGH. By Colonel Sir WILLIAM BUTLER.

SIR JOHN MOORE. By Colonel MAURICE.

MACMILLAN AND CO., LONDON.

www.ingramcontent.com/pod-product-compliance
Lightning Source LLC
Chambersburg PA
CBHW021409230426
43666CB00006B/683